LA
CUISINE

Also by Diana and Paul von Welanetz:

The Art of Buffet Entertaining

*Celebrations: A Menu Cookbook
for Informal Entertaining*

The Pleasure of Your Company

The von Welanetz Guide to Ethnic Ingredients

With Love from Your Kitchen

LA CUISINE

the new culinary spirit

Diana and Paul von Welanetz

recipes and menus from the celebrated chefs of los angeles

JEREMY P. TARCHER, INC.
Los Angeles
Distributed by Houghton Mifflin Company
Boston

Acknowledgments

The following people have been invaluable and a joy in many ways, some with recipes, and some with inspiration and support: Janice Gallagher, our esteemed editor; Mary Charles, Craig Claiborne, Pat Connell, Marion Cunningham, Derek Gallagher, Luci Goodman of Sussman/Prejza, Tracy Goss and the entire staff of Impact Studios, Linda and Ray Hege, Pauline Kelbly, Candance Kommers, Steve Koffler, Eileen and Norman Kreiss, Julie and Michael Loshin of Parties Plus, Lana Marder, John and Katie Marin, Dick Mount, Joan Nielsen, Kay Okrand, Jeanette Marie Paulsen, Frances and Jimmy Pelham, Chef Paul Prudhomme, for recipes from *Chef Paul Prudhomme's Louisiana Kitchen*, Wolfgang Puck, Sheila and Michael Ricci, Lynn Robbins, Terry Roseman, Mimi and Jack Schneider, John Sedlar, Piero Selvaggio, Tom Sewell, Doris Shaw, Judi Skalsky, Sandra Stoff of Princess Cruises, Claudia and Russ Stromberg, Tommy Tang, Jeremy Tarcher, Maggie Waldron, Wilmer Weiss, Lexi von Welanetz, Marge Welanetz, Robert Willson, Leslie Wilshire.

Library of Congress Cataloging in Publication Data

Von Welanetz, Diana.
  L.A. cuisine.

  Includes index.
    1. Cookery – California – Los Angeles. 2. Los Angeles (Calif.) – Social
       customs. 3. Los Angeles (Calif.) – Restaurants. I. Von Welanetz,
Paul. II. Title. III. Title: LA cuisine.
TX715.V79 1985   641.5'09794'93   85-4645
ISBN 0-87477-361-X

Requests for such permissions should be addressed to:

Jeremy P. Tarcher, Inc.
9110 Sunset Blvd.
Los Angeles, CA 90069

Manufactured in the United States of America

A 10 9 8 7 6 5 4 3 2 1

First Edition

Contents

A California Cuisine Dinner for 6 to 8   38

Pizza with Eggplant, Sun-Dried Tomatoes, Feta, and Mint

Chicken Breasts in Garlic Parmesan Cream
on a bed of Fresh Zucchini and Carrot Pasta, Gremolata Garnish

Carrot Flowers with Green Bean Stems

Hot Apricot Soufflé

Dinner for 6 at Sheila and Michael Ricci's   50

Zucchini Madeleines

Garden Salad with Fresh Corn and Balsamic Vinegar Dressing

Stuffed Leg of Lamb with Sherried Brown Sauce and Wild Mushrooms

Roasted Yellow, Red, and Green Peppers

Irish Oatmeal Bread

English Manor House Pie with Two Creams

Kay Okrand's Menu for a Summer Buffet for 20   63

Basket of Raw and Al Dente Vegetables with Sun-Dried Tomato and
Basil Mayonnaise

Chicken Piccata

Stir-Fried Vegetables in Fresh Herb Butter

Pasta Primavera Salad

Five-Leaf Salad

Focaccia with Fresh Rosemary

Amaretto Chiffon Cheesecake in a Macaroon Crust

Long-Stemmed Strawberries Dipped in White and Dark Chocolates

Espresso and Cappuccino

A Quick and Fresh Vegetarian Supper for 6   80

Belgian Endive with Hazelnut Mayonnaise Dip

Avocado Pasta with Green Beans and Fresh Tomato Sauce

Black Cherry Sorbet with Dark Rum
or Fresh Fruit with California Zabaglione

A Catered Menu for 30   88

Hors d'oeuvres passed on trays:

Asparagus Tempura with Apricot Mustard

Potato and Carrot Pancakes with Melting Brie and Poached Pears

Spicy Shrimp with California Salsa

Pizza with Smoked Duck, Blue Cheese, and Red Onions

Roasted Garlic with Dill Toast Points

Breast of Chicken Stuffed with Wild Mushroom Duxelles,
Grilled over Mesquite

Mélange of Grilled Vegetables

Garlic Fettuccine Tossed with Roasted Red Peppers and Fresh Basil

Crisp Herb Bread with Tomato Butter

White Chocolate Charlotte with Raspberry Puree and
Bittersweet Chocolate Sauce

The L.A. Restaurant Style   110

Les Anges   114

Poisson aux Trois Citrons (Fish with Three Citrus Fruits)
Sole au Vin Rouge (Sole in Red Wine Sauce)

Bernard's   117
Les Coquilles St.-Jacques à la Vapeur
(Steamed Scallops with Vermouth Sauce)

Bistango   119
Salmis de Canard au Zinfandel et aux Champignons Sauvages
(Duck Breasts in Zinfandel Sauce with Wild Mushrooms)

Le Chardonnay   122
Warm Sweetbread Salad with Snow Peas and Oyster Mushrooms

La Petite Chaya and Chaya Brasserie   124
Cigares de Poulet au Curry à la Chaya
(Baked Spring Rolls Stuffed with Chicken and Mushrooms)

Chinois on Main   127
Sizzling Catfish

City Cafe   129
Grilled Chicken with Bulgur

La Cucina   132
Angel Hair Pasta with Fresh Tomato and Basil Sauce

Cutters   133
Yaki Soba with Chicken

Katsu   136
Red Snapper Stuffed with Tofu

Michael's   139
Chicken and Goat Cheese Salad

Muse   141
Chocolate Gâteau Mousseline

Nowhere Cafe   143
Grilled Chicken Breasts with Salsa Puchol

Orleans   145
Hot Fanny Sauce
Sweet Potato Pecan Pie

Palette   150
Spicy Shrimp in Cellophane

How This Book Is Organized

We would like to say a word or two here about how this book is organized. The first half consists of menus for entertaining, including some of our own and some menus from our favorite hosts and caterers. They reflect the current styles of entertaining at home in Los Angeles. Timetables are given for party planning, as well as tips for making all these recipes ahead of time.

The second half of the book is a compilation of those restaurants which, in our opinion, best represent the current trends in Los Angeles, along with a few of their signature recipes. We chose them not because they are considered the "best", though many of them are, but because they demonstrate the unique Los Angeles style. The city is changing rapidly, and restaurants come and go; nevertheless, these are well worth noting for the impact we believe they are having on our food-consciousness.

To Los Angeles,
crossroads of the Western World,
and her infinite possibilities

L.A. Cuisine

Los Angeles has developed its own cuisine based on its climate and geography, its enormous population of every known ethnicity, its abundance of fresh produce, and the sophistication of its diners and chefs. While the East Coast is the entry port for Europe, the West Coast is a magnet for the Orient, and has, as well, a direct connection with the immense land mass of Latin America.

The city comprises 140 communities housing 13 million people of every imaginable ethnic background. No other area in the Western world has such ethnic intermingling. The population is 52 percent minority. It is the place where East meets West, where Southwest and Mexico filter in, where Italian, French, and Middle Eastern influences intersect.

Let's explore the development of the New American Cuisine, so that we can better understand what is happening in Los Angeles. During the 60's there was a rebellion against the canned and chemically treated foods that were born of necessity during the First and Second World Wars. Americans wanted "real" food instead of convenience, and, with the help of Julia Child and others, began to pursue it by studying classic French cooking techniques. At the beginning of the 70's the cuisine of France was mired in 300 years of dependence on fewer than 100 basic recipes, such as *Oeufs en gelée, Quenelles de brochet,* and *Filet de boeuf Richelieu,* and chefs were becoming bored with *la cuisine classique.* It was then, out of a desire to rediscover what food really tastes like, that France discovered the Orient. Embracing the simplicity, the textures and color contrasts, and the lightness of Oriental cuisine, and using fresh, local ingredients, the French created *la nouvelle cuisine.* It was a cuisine *du marché* – of the market – which took what was fresh each day, prepared it simply, and allowed its natural beauty to be its own best presentation.

Inspired by nouvelle cuisine, eager young professional chefs everywhere, well-grounded in classic techniques, cast aside the rigidity of the old rules and began to experiment. Nouvelle cuisine itself quickly became a thing of the past as cooks and chefs started to play with ingredients available at ethnic markets. Throughout the United States newly stylized regional cuisines began to develop around local ingredients. Los Angeles, long a major trendsetter for the rest of the country, fashioned its own version of East-meets-West with "Franco-Japonaise," "Chinoise," and what might be termed "Franco-Santa Fe" dishes.

Our Mediterranean climate and geographic location provide a year-round abundance of fresh produce, making California the nation's largest single agricultural state – with a 1-billion-dollar annual industry. Angeleno cooks have a unique advantage. All kinds of morning-fresh produce and herbs are found in the steadily growing number of local farmer's markets, and locally produced cheeses and wines are far too numerous to count. Artichokes, avocados, and dates, long considered California ingredients, are making room in the markets for sunchokes, arugula, and radicchio; fresh oyster, shiitake, and chanterelle mushrooms; Finnish butter potatoes and California goat cheese. The cottage industries that provide many of these foodstuffs help to give Los Angeles chefs a vital cutting edge, inspiring spontaneity and innovativeness. Our local cuisine has become a montage of Asian, Old World European, Latin American, and American Indian, blended with the rigid discipline of codified French techniques. The up-to-date Los Angeles chef expresses culinary innovativeness through skillful sautés, crisp, colorful stir-fries, and perfect mixed grills smoldering over Southwestern mesquite.

Increased consumption of chicken and fish and decreased consumption of red meats are the result of a typically Californian concern with health and fitness. Legumes, whole grains, and fresh fruits and vegetables, once fare for natural food buffs, are now on sophisticated menus everywhere. The focus is on the quality of life, and the motivation to return to basics is at the heart of Los Angeles' interest in food.

The freeway-connected communities of Los Angeles support 17,000 restaurants, far more per capita than any other city. Dining out, not so surprisingly, has become a popular new form of recreation in a city busy discovering, tasting, and adapting new cuisines. Challenged to stay one step ahead of sophisticated customers, chefs take advantage of a rich diversity of ingredients, including new strains of vegetables continually being developed by truck farmers who grow specifically for choosy restaurateurs. There is an ever-increasing demand for better and newer raw ingredients, and these spark the chefs' imaginations to create completely new food combinations. We now expect the unexpected.

Kipling was wrong, culinarily at least. East has met West. In fact, that meeting is currently taking place in Los Angeles. The result is a thriving and exuberant L.A. cuisine.

How L.A. Entertains
at Home

Contemporary hospitality is being studied, analyzed, and reviewed on all fronts today – social, psychological, aesthetic, financial, industrial. It is an art that translates importantly in the American marketplace. As a husband-and-wife team we have explored this art for more than twenty years from our base in Los Angeles. We have traveled and lived all over the world, observing different cultures and studying the art of hospitality, cooking, and the history of food. But our teaching philosophy has been importantly shaped in Los Angeles. And why not? Californians have long been among the forerunners in the design of better living.

Hospitality and the joy of sharing are a deep and natural part of our culture. They are among our finest instincts. In the 80's, entertaining at home, like so many other activities, is breaking away from the old formulas. One reason is that women are entering the workforce in ever-increasing numbers, so they have less free time. We have smaller living spaces, less household help, but more spendable dollars. The kitchen is often the focal point of the house and guests frequently join in the cooking; it would seem that people want more than ever to be with other people. To escape the high-tech stress of our lives we want to entertain at home, but not according to the rigid rules handed down to us by our parents. The new form of entertaining might be compared to a spontaneous improvisational dance, rather than the tight structure of a ballet.

One solution Angelenos have found to providing appropriate food for a gathering is to buy it at the ever-increasing number of fine food emporia. Gourmet-to-go is becoming the hottest new business of the decade, with even "from scratch" cooks often standing in line to purchase tastefully prepared dishes that meet their own standards. One can find a source for just about any prepared food from sushi to French pastry. First-rate restaurants are, more and more, making their specialties available for take-out. It's expensive, but the cost is weighed against time saved. Our friends Eileen and Norman Kreiss buy complete menus from such an establishment, the new St. Germain To Go. They are able to serve business lunches in the comfortable environment of their furniture showroom, combining the convenience of dining out with the graciousness of a home dining room.

The world is getting smaller, and what used to be exotic foods are finding easy acceptance in supermarkets: kielbasa, feta cheese, jalapeños, tortillas, and tofu are common names to shoppers. Baklava, the Greek sweetmeat made of paper-thin sheets of filo pastry, nuts, and honey, continues to be one of the most popular take-out foods from ethnic delis, but enthusiastic cooks like to use the very versatile filo for all sorts of improvisational cooking as well, using it to wrap lamb chops, vegetable terrines, fruit pies, and so on.

The natural foods movement of the 60's, combined with the fitness movement of the past decade, has made Californians very aware of food quality and good nutrition. Most often, fresh and simple is the key, for the finer the ingredients the less complicated the preparation need be. Fine-quality vegetables are sought out at farmer's markets

6

along with locally produced cheeses and wines, and these are the foundation of the new style of cooking. For instance, a salad featuring a variety of baby greens, simply dressed with flavorful oils and vinegars, might be followed by an herb-marinated grilled chicken or fish accompanied by lightly stir-fried vegetables; California cheese, crusty bread, and fresh local berries make a suitable finish.

Time saved in cooking is often spent on the look of the tabletop and the arrangement of food on the plate. A growing number of new craft galleries are featuring functional works of art such as handmade dishes and bowls that must be used to be fully admired. At-home entertaining can combine the best of two worlds: the food can be presented as handsomely as it would be in a fine restaurant, while the diners enjoy the pleasures of a more relaxed and more personal style of cuisine.

Following are examples of Los Angeles-style menus that represent what we and some of our friends who love to entertain are preparing for guests these days.

East Meets West Menu for 8 to 10

*Raw Vegetables with Ginger Aïoli
Served in a Chinese Bamboo Steamer*

Peking Pizza

Chenin Blanc

or

Sauvignon Blanc

*Shark, Tuna, or Salmon Grilled over Mesquite
with Fresh Herb Butter, Garnished with Herb
Flowers*

Chardonnay

or

Sauvignon Blanc

Grilled Vegetables

Mango or Peach Sorbet

Espresso

Meals we prepare for friends often center on grilled main courses – fish, chicken, or meat, and the vegetables that accompany them. The cooking method is easy, and our guests enjoy watching the preparation and even having a part in the process. One guest might baste fish with olive oil, while another tosses a salad, turns vegetables with tongs, or passes an appetizer.

Mesquite and other hardwoods, used in restaurants for grilling both for flavor and for their long-burning characteristics, are not really practical for home use. Mesquite chips or briquettes are found in almost every market, however, along with portable grills or braziers that can even be used on top of the kitchen stove under a vent. We agree with many of L.A.'s top chefs that more delicately flavored fish, such as flounder, are overpowered by the strong flavor of mesquite, but we find that it does enhance the flavors of the more assertively flavored shark, tuna, or salmon recommended in this menu. Cooking vegetables on the grill along with the main course gives them a special smoky flavor as well.

This simple grilling of meat and vegetables is not unlike the *robata* cooking of Japan, country-style grilling of fresh seasonal foods, and it is a reminder of the Orient's profound impact on the foods we love to prepare in Los Angeles. We are continually inspired by the array of Oriental ingredients and produce widely available at almost every supermarket.

Bamboo steamer baskets make attractive containers for raw or blanched vegetables, to be dipped into a gingery, garlicky mayonnaise and nibbled during the preparation. (If we can get baby vegetables at the Wednesday farmer's market in Santa Monica, so much the better.) The center of attention, though, is a dish containing Chinese roast duck. Purchased at one of the many delis located along Broadway in Chinatown and stored in the freezer for improvisational use, the duck sparked our imagination, resulting in an unusual appetizer combining the flavors found in that much-loved restaurant dish, Peking Duck, with the West Coast's passion for pizza.

The menu becomes simpler as it progresses, a style we've adapted from Roy Yamaguchi, owner/chef of 385 North, who serves the heavier and more complex dishes at the beginning of a meal. Thyme and rosemary grow year-round in our garden, so we use their leaves to infuse a fragrant herb butter for the fish while their flowers become a simple garnish. Any butter that makes its way onto the grilled Japanese eggplant and other vegetables will only enhance their flavor.

Dessert, uncomplicated too, is a fresh fruit sorbet garnished with strips of tangerine or lime rind and accompanied by a cup of espresso.

Timetable

A week or more ahead:

Make and freeze pizza dough.

Buy duck and freeze.

Freeze herb butter.

One day ahead:

Cook artichoke.

Prepare aïoli dip and vegetables for dipping.

Up to 8 hours ahead:

Thaw pizza dough, if frozen.

Prepare pizza toppings.

Prepare sorbet.

Prepare citrus rind to garnish sorbet.

Chill wines.

An hour before guests arrive:

Marinate fish.

Assemble and bake pizza.

Assemble vegetables with dip; spray with water to preserve freshness.

After guests arrive:

Grill vegetables and fish.

Brew espresso.

Raw Vegetables with Ginger Aïoli Served in a Chinese Bamboo Steamer 10 or more servings

Chinese steamers made of bamboo are available inexpensively in cookware shops and department stores, and we use them often as serving baskets. The idea for adding ginger to aïoli (garlic mayonnaise) came from San Francisco food expert Maggie Waldron. Our Los Angeles-style aïoli is a quick rather than a traditional version.

large artichoke, to hold the dip

Raw Vegetables (buy amount and variety desired):

Jícama, peeled and cut into spears with a serrated cutter

Zucchini, cut into diagonal slices with a serrated cutter

Carrots, peeled and cut into thin diagonal slices

Sugar snap peas, stringed but left whole

Red, green, yellow, and purple bell peppers (available at specialty produce markets), cored, seeded, and cut into strips

Broccoli florets, blanched (see Note)

Brussels sprouts, blanched and halved

Cauliflower florets, blanched

Tiny red or white potatoes, cooked in their skins until tender

Ginger Aïoli (makes 2 cups):

4   *slices (the size of a quarter) peeled fresh ginger*

2   *garlic cloves*

¼   *cup dry breadcrumbs, made from French or Italian bread*

2   *teaspoons fresh lemon juice*

Pinch of cayenne pepper

2   *cups homemade or commercial mayonnaise*

Note: Some raw vegetables benefit by blanching to heighten their color and make them more tender. To blanch, drop the cut vegetables into rapidly boiling water for about 10 to 60 seconds, until crisp-tender; blanch each vegetable separately. Transfer with a slotted spoon to ice water. When cool, dry on paper towels. Prepare other vegetables as listed; cover and refrigerate.

Trim the artichoke stem flush with the bottom. Use scissors to trim ¼ inch off the point of each leaf. Rinse artichoke and steam for 30 to 45 minutes, or until the bottom is tender when pierced with a fork. Drain and cool. Spread the top leaves apart until you see the tiny leaves covering the hairy choke. Scrape away the leaves and choke using a small teaspoon or grapefruit spoon. Place a small glass or ramekin in the hollow to hold the dip.

To make the aïoli, combine ginger and garlic in food processor fitted with the steel blade; process until minced. Add the breadcrumbs, lemon juice, cayenne pepper, and mayonnaise and process until blended. Let stand for at least an hour so that breadcrumbs thicken the mixture and the flavor of the ginger develops fully.

Spoon the dip into the center of the cooked artichoke. Place in the center of a steamer basket and surround with other vegetables for dipping.

To prepare in advance: Ginger aïoli will keep for a week or longer in the refrigerator, tightly covered. The artichoke may be cooked and the vegetables prepared a day ahead. Wrap in damp paper towels, place in plastic bags, and refrigerate.

Peking Pizza
**Makes one 12-inch pizza
8 to 10 appetizer servings**

We've experimented with many pizza doughs, and this quick and simple one is our favorite. Bake pizza either on a heavy pizza pan that has been sprinkled with cornmeal, or on a pizza stone or *unglazed* quarry tile that has been preheated in the oven for half an hour. Either method absorbs moisture from the dough and creates a crisp crust.

Deliciously seasoned Cantonese-style roast duck is sold by weight, whole or in pieces, at Chinatown barbecued-meat markets or delis. Take a large plastic bag with you when purchasing these, as the take-home containers tend to leak. Roast duck is one of the most versatile ingredients possible to have on hand for impromptu cooking. The discovery of a round of pizza dough and a Chinese duck in our freezer led to this successful improvisation.

Basic Pizza Crust:

2   *cups bread flour or unbleached all-purpose flour*

2   *teaspoons sugar*

½   *teaspoon salt*

1½   *teaspoons (½ package) active dry yeast*

⅔   *cup warm water (105° to 115°F)*

1   *tablespoon olive oil*

    Cornmeal for the pan

Peking Topping:

1   *tablespoon sesame oil*

3   *tablespoons* hoisin *sauce*

1   *tablespoon minced fresh ginger*

1   *bunch scallions (including some of the green tops), thinly sliced*

1 tablespoon toasted sesame seed

½ a Chinese roast duck, meat shredded and skin reserved

6 *fresh* shiitake *mushrooms, sliced, or dried* shiitake, *soaked, squeezed, and sliced (discard stems)*

8 ounces part-skim mozzarella cheese, shredded
reserved pieces of duck skin

1 tablespoon finely chopped fresh coriander (cilantro),
to garnish

For crust, combine the flour, sugar, and salt in a mixing bowl or food processor and blend briefly. Sprinkle yeast into water, then stir until dissolved. Add olive oil to the yeast mixture. If mixing by hand, add the liquid gradually to the flour mixture while stirring with a wooden spoon, then turn the dough out onto a lightly floured surface and knead until smooth and satiny, about 3 to 4 minutes. If using a food processor, turn machine on and pour the liquid through the feed tube, processing until the dough forms a ball. Knead it in the machine for 30 seconds or so, then turn dough out onto a lightly floured surface.

Place rack in bottom third of oven and preheat the oven to 425° F for 30 minutes, with pizza stone or tile if using it. Cover the dough with a large bowl and let it rest for 15 to 30 minutes. Lightly sprinkle a heavy pizza pan, baking sheet, or wooden "peel" (paddle used to slide pizza onto hot oven tile) lightly with cornmeal. Press dough into a flat disc, then stretch with hands into a 12-inch circle. Place on pan or peel, brush with sesame oil, and let rest for 15 to 30 minutes.

Arrange remaining topping ingredients over the dough in the order listed, leaving a 1-inch margin all around and reserving coriander for garnish. Bake at 425°F for approximately 20 minutes, or until the crust is browned and the duck skin is very crisp. Sprinkle with coriander. Let rest 10 minutes, then use a pizza wheel to cut into wedges.

To prepare in advance: Chinese duck freezes well for up to 4 months, and need only be thawed before use in recipe. The pizza may be baked several hours ahead and reheated for serving, but flavor and texture are at their best when pizza is freshly baked.

Shark, Tuna, or Salmon Grilled over Mesquite with Fresh Herb Butter, Garnished with Herb Flowers
8 to 10 servings

Many California homes and condominiums are landscaped with pine-needled rosemary or one of many varieties of thyme, both of which sport pale lavender flowers. We like to use the herb flowers to garnish grilled meats, as they are attractive, edible and very fragrant. Fresh herbs are also sold in bunches in most supermarkets, often with the tiny flowers attached. If flowers are not available, a small amount of the minced fresh herb will do.

Herb Butter:

¼ *cup chopped fresh herbs, such as thyme, rosemary, and/or chives*

¾ *cup (1½ sticks) butter, softened*

2 *tablespoons fresh lemon juice*

Salt to taste

Freshly ground black pepper to taste

8 *to 10 shark, tuna or salmon steaks, 6 to 8 ounces each*

About ⅓ cup olive oil

Freshly ground black pepper

Flowering thyme, rosemary, or chives, if available (see Note)

Note: Rosemary is a very pungent herb, and should be used only on such strongly flavored fish as those recommended in this menu.

To make herb butter, reserve any flowers from the herbs for garnish. Chop the herbs with a knife or in food processor fitted with the steel blade.

Mix in the softened butter and lemon juice. Use a rubber spatula to transfer the mixture to a piece of waxed paper or foil, distributing it evenly in a log about 1 inch in diameter. Wrap into a smooth roll and chill at least 2 hours, or until serving time.

Marinate the fish steaks for at least 10 minutes in the olive oil with a sprinkling of black pepper. Place them, if desired, in a grilling basket for ease of handling, and grill over hot coals for 6 to 8 minutes, turning once and basting with olive oil mixture. Serve immediately, first-cooked side up, on hot plates. Unwrap the chilled herb butter and cut into 10 even slices, placing one on each serving of fish. Sprinkle each serving lightly with herb flowers or minced fresh herbs.

To prepare in advance: Fresh herb butters freeze well for months if wrapped airtight, and are great to have on hand for all kinds of grilled meats and poultry, as well as the more flavorful fish. Grilling should take place just before serving.

Grilled Vegetables 8 to 10 servings

These colorful vegetables require only about 10 minutes to cook, and may be kept warm in a low oven while the fish is cooked to the desired doneness.

8   to 10 small Japanese eggplant (see Note)

5   brown onions, halved, with skins

4   to 5 red and/or green bell peppers, seeds and
    membranes removed, halved

3   crookneck squash, cut diagonally into ½-inch slices

    About 40 sugar snap peas, strings removed

Note: If not available, cut a 1-pound eggplant into
8 to 10 lengthwise wedges, brushing cut sides with
olive oil.

Place the whole eggplants and halved onions directly
on the grill for about 5 minutes, then add the bell
peppers and squash slices. Turn the vegetables as
they begin to char. The peas should go on last, and
will require only a minute or so to warm them through.

To prepare in advance: Arrange the vegetables on hot
serving plates or on a platter that may be covered
with foil and kept warm in a low oven until serving
time.

Mango or Peach Sorbet Makes 1 quart

The addition of liqueur keeps this sorbet soft and
spoonable for up to 8 hours.

2   to 3 ripe mangoes or *peaches, to make 2 cups puree*

½   cup sugar

2   cups water

3   tablespoons fresh lemon juice

1   tablespoon Grand Marnier or *Kirsch*

If not using an electric ice cream maker:

1   egg white

1   tablespoon sugar

Garnish

Grated rind of 1 lime or tangerine

Peel and pit the mangoes or peaches. Place the pulp in a blender or food processor and process to a smooth puree.

Combine sugar and water in a small saucepan, bring to a boil and simmer for 5 minutes. Cool completely.

If making in an electric ice cream maker: Combine fruit puree, sugar syrup, lemon juice, and liqueur and pour into electric ice cream maker. Freeze according to manufacturer's directions.

If making without an electric ice cream maker: Beaten egg white must be added to keep large ice crystals from forming during the freezing. Combine fruit puree and sugar syrup. Beat egg white until soft peaks form, then gradually beat in the 1 tablespoon sugar to form stiff peaks. Fold into the fruit mixture. Turn into a shallow metal pan, cover with plastic wrap, and freeze for 2 to 3 hours, or until mushy. Transfer sorbet to electric mixer and beat in lemon juice and liqueur until sorbet is soft and fluffy. Return to pan. Freeze 1 hour longer, or until firm. Spoon sorbet into serving glasses and top each serving with grated citrus rind.

To prepare in advance: A sorbet must be prepared within a few hours of serving or it becomes too icy to scoop. If very hard, remove it from the freezer to soften for 15 minutes before scooping. Prepare rind for garnish up to 8 hours ahead. Cover with damp paper towels and store in refrigerator until serving time.

A Southwestern Brunch for 10 to 12

Fresh Honeydew Daiquiris

or

Iced Tea with Pineapple Spears and Fresh Mint

Paella Salad with Grilled Chorizo

Brisket Braised in Red Wine with Ancho Chile Sauce

Scrambled Eggs in Red Bell Pepper Shells

Apple Tostadas

Almond Coffee (made from flavored beans)

To introduce this menu, we would like to tell you about our own lifestyle, our home, and how we entertain, so that you will better understand our participation in the new Los Angeles culinary spirit.

It was 10 years ago that we moved into our present home in the town of Pacific Palisades, which is located on the ocean between Santa Monica and Malibu. Some people give names to their houses, and if we had to name ours it would be The Treehouse. Center-front there is a huge old sycamore tree around which the architect (bless him) built the entryway. From all the front windows we see this graceful tree through the seasons (Easterners claim that California doesn't have seasons, but we do – two of them) and a visitor has the feeling that the house is a part of the tree. On the opposite side of the house, through the living room, is an expansive redwood deck and dining patio overlooking a canyon that fans open to the ocean. On most days we see the island of Catalina right in the entrance to our canyon opening. Being at the end of a cul-de-sac, we are blessed with little traffic. It is very private and quiet, an ideal home for two writers and a 16-year-old daughter. It is always surprising to out-of-town guests that one can live in this huge city and enjoy an uncrowded, country feeling. This is the Los Angeles visitors rarely see.

The kitchen was not practical for two cooks when we bought the house, so Paul redesigned it, moved the refrigerator, and built a 12-foot chopping block countertop around two sides to give us lots of work space and a place to serve kitchen buffets. The windows above this L-shaped area look over a tiled patio, a fence with pots of herbs, and the canyon-ocean view beyond. We've always been grateful, especially when washing dishes, that the architect gave the best view in the house to the kitchen, where we spend so many of our hours together and with friends.

Our usual style of entertaining is informal, and we concentrate on creating menus we can prepare ahead of time and serve without help. Brunch lends itself beautifully to our informality, being an uncomplicated meal. And both guests and hosts are fresh and relaxed on weekend mornings. This menu is a good example of Los Angeles style, for we are greatly influenced by the large Latino population, and interest in all kinds of Mexican, Tex-Mex, and Southwestern foods is flourishing.

Timetable

Two days ahead:

Prepare rice mixture for salad.

Cook brisket and chill.

Prepare apples and grate cheese for tostadas.

Up to 8 hours ahead:

Prepare melon and garnish for daiquiris or iced tea.

Slice brisket; top with sauce.

Char bell pepper shells.

An hour before guests arrive:

Blend daiquiris, if desired.

Garnish paella salad.

Brew almond coffee.

Fry tortillas for tostadas.

After guests arrive:

Blend daiquiris if not pre-done.

Reheat brisket for 45 minutes.

Assemble tostadas.

Scramble eggs.

Honeydew Daiquiris **Makes 3 large drinks**

This smooth, pale green drink is light on alcohol and ideal for daytime parties. Usually we can cajole one of our guests into making and serving these.

½ *blender container of shaved ice* or *small ice cubes*

¼ *large (about 2 pounds before peeling) ripe honeydew melon, peeled, seeded, and cubed*

2 *ounces (¼ cup) light rum*

1 *ounce (2 tablespoons) Midori melon liqueur*

3 *ounces (6 tablespoons) frozen lemonade concentrate (do not thaw)*

Garnish:

A small wedge of honeydew, slice of lime, or strawberry for each glass

Combine all ingredients except garnish in blender container and blend until smooth and slushy. Pour into large margarita glasses, brandy snifters, or other stemmed glasses. Decorate each drink with a small wedge of honeydew, a lime slice, or a strawberry, by making a slit in the fruit and hanging it on the rim of the glass.

To prepare in advance: After blending, the drink may be held in the freezer for several hours if necessary; it won't freeze solid because of its alcohol content. Reblend just before serving.

Paella Salad with Grilled Chorizo
12 servings

This dish of bright yellow rice studded with sausages, shrimp, and colorful vegetables is one of the most eye-appealing salads we've ever devised.

<table>
</table>

Handwritten	Qty	Ingredient

x 4

2 cooked chickens (approximately 2 pounds each), skinned while warm

7 + 2 water   4½ cups chicken broth

4   2 cups raw long-grain rice

each pot   *3*   1½ teaspoons fresh thyme leaves, finely chopped, or ½ teaspoon dried thyme, crumbled

2   1 teaspoon saffron threads, crumbled, or ¼ teaspoon powdered saffron (see Note 1)

½   ¼ teaspoon (or more) turmeric

2 C   ½ cup light olive oil or vegetable oil ✓

12 T   3 tablespoons red wine vinegar ✓

4   1 medium garlic clove, minced ✓

2 t.   ½ teaspoon salt ✓

Freshly ground black pepper to taste

12 large cooked shrimp, shelled and deveined

8 ounces Spanish chorizo, grilled and sliced diagonally (see Note 2)

6 baby artichokes, cooked until tender and halved, or 1 package (10 ounces) frozen artichoke hearts, cooked according to package directions

1 cup fresh peas, shelled and cooked in simmering water just until tender, or frozen tiny peas, thawed

1 cup diced red bell pepper

1 bunch scallions (including most of the green tops), sliced

½ cup toasted slivered almonds

½ cup minced fresh parsley

12 pitted black olives, halved

Garnish:

1 head romaine lettuce

2 medium tomatoes, cut into wedges

Note 1: Saffron threads may be purchased in small glass vials at many ethnic markets, fish stores, and supermarkets. Powdered saffron, generally more expensive, is available in glass jars at most supermarkets. You may have to ask the manager for it, as it is stored in a dark place.

Note 2: Spanish chorizo is made with smoked pork and formed into firm sausages that are much more easily sliced than the Mexican type, which tends to be crumbly. You may use any garlic-flavored sausage you like, even Polish kielbasa.

Bone the chickens and cut any very large pieces into bite-size morsels. Refrigerate.

Combine chicken broth, rice, thyme, saffron, and turmeric in a heavy 4-to 5-quart saucepan. Bring to a simmer, then cover tightly and simmer over very low heat for 25 minutes without lifting the lid. Check to see if the rice has absorbed the liquid and, if necessary, cover and cook a bit longer. Remove from heat; transfer to a mixing bowl. Shake the oil, vinegar, garlic, salt, and pepper together in a small jar and pour over the rice, tossing to coat evenly. Refrigerate at least 2 hours.

Just before serving, fold chicken pieces and remaining salad ingredients into chilled rice mixture. Heap decoratively into a large gratin dish or paella pan which has been lined with romaine lettuce leaves. Garnish with tomato wedges.

To prepare in advance: The marinated rice mixture may be prepared several days ahead and kept chilled. For maximum freshness, add the remaining ingredients within 2 hours of serving; keep chilled.

Brisket Braised in Red Wine with Ancho Chile Sauce 12 to 16 servings

An improvisation on one of our family's favorite brisket recipes; the sauce is thickened with pureed vegetables, not with flour. By adding red chile sauce and Mexican seasonings we've created a whole new dish with a Southwestern flavor.

1   *lean beef brisket (6 pounds)*

　　Salt and freshly ground black pepper to taste

6   *medium-size brown onions, chopped*

4   *carrots, peeled and sliced into ½-inch lengths*

4   *garlic cloves, minced or pressed*

2½ *cups dry red wine*

3½ *cups Mexican red chile sauce (see Note)*

2   *tablespoons tomato paste*

2   *teaspoons chili powder*

1   *teaspoon dried oregano, crumbled*

½   *teaspoon ground cumin*

1   *teaspoon fresh lemon juice*

Optional Garnish:

1   *cup sour cream*

　　Leaves from a small bunch of fresh coriander (cilantro)

1   *ripe avocado, peeled, pitted, and cut lengthwise into thin wedges*

Note: This is nothing like the popular chili sauce displayed next to the catsup bottles in every supermarket. It is a Mexican sauce made from the pureed pulp of dried red chiles cooked with various spices, and is used on enchiladas or as a table sauce for tacos or tostadas. Conveniently, a canned version is available in

most Southern California supermarkets under the Las Palmas label, or you can make your own in the following manner: Heat 6 ounces washed and dried, whole dried red chiles (ancho, New Mexico, or California) briefly on a dry griddle or in a skillet just until softened (take care not to scorch the chiles as you warm them, or they will taste very bitter). Remove stem, seeds, and veins. Tear chiles into pieces and place in a medium saucepan. Add 3 cups water and bring just to a simmer. Remove from heat and let stand 1 hour. Drain chiles, reserving soaking liquid. Place ⅓ to ½ the chiles in the container of a blender or food processor with 2 garlic cloves, 1 teaspoon salt, 1½ teaspoons chopped fresh oregano (or ½ teaspoon dried oregano, crumbled), ½ teaspoon ground cumin, and just enough of the soaking liquid to keep the mixture moving through the blades. Process until pureed and return to the soaking liquid. Repeat with remaining chiles. Strain the mixture through a medium-mesh strainer, pressing dry and discarding any pulp left in the strainer. Measure liquid and add water if necessary to make 4 cups. Transfer to a saucepan, add 2 tablespoons lard or vegetable oil, and simmer for 10 minutes, stirring often. Add 2 to 3 teaspoons red wine vinegar and season with salt and freshly ground pepper to taste.

Preheat oven to 500°F.

Sprinkle the brisket generously with salt and pepper and place it fat side up in a heavy roasting pan or Dutch oven. Roast uncovered for 25 to 35 minutes, or until nicely browned. Sprinkle onions and carrots evenly over the meat. Stir together the garlic, wine, red chile sauce, tomato paste, chili powder, oregano, and cumin. Pour the liquid around the meat and cover the pan. Lower oven temperature to 325°F and continue cooking for 4 hours or longer, until meat is very tender.

Lift the meat from the liquid and allow to rest for 20 minutes before slicing. Meanwhile, strain the sauce, reserving both solids and liquid. Place the solids in a blender or food mill and process to a smooth sauce, adding enough reserved liquid to thin the sauce to the desired consistency.

To serve, carve the meat, not too thinly, across the grain. Arrange the slices on a warm platter and spoon sauce over them to coat evenly. Garnish, if desired, with sour cream, cilantro leaves, and thin wedges of avocado. Serve extra sauce on the side.

To prepare in advance: This dish may be cooked several days ahead. Cool the meat to room temperature, cover, and refrigerate. It may be sliced when cold, arranged in a serving dish, and covered with sauce; reheat at 325°F for about 45 minutes.

Scrambled Eggs in Red Bell Pepper Shells 12 servings

Lightly charred bell pepper halves make colorful containers for individual servings of scrambled eggs.

6 *small red bell peppers*

2 *dozen eggs*

½ *cup cream* or *milk*

   Salt and freshly ground black pepper

¼ *cup (½ stick) butter* or *bacon drippings*

2 *tablespoons minced fresh parsley* or *snipped chives*

12 *sprigs parsley* or *fresh coriander* (cilantro), *to garnish*

Preheat broiler. Cut bell peppers in half lengthwise through the stem; remove seeds and membranes. Place cut side down on a baking sheet. Place peppers about 3 inches from heat and watch closely until lightly charred. Set aside.

Break eggs into a medium bowl, add cream and salt and pepper, and beat with a whisk until frothy. Heat butter or bacon drippings in a very large skillet, add eggs, and cook and stir over medium heat for about 4 minutes, or until firm but still very creamy. Just before they are done, stir in the parsley or chives.

Arrange the bell pepper halves cut side up on a warm serving platter. Divide the scrambled eggs among the shells and garnish each with parsley or fresh coriander.

To prepare in advance: Prepare bell pepper shells up to 8 hours before serving; leave at room temperature. Scramble eggs just before serving.

Apple Tostadas 12 servings

Brunch requires no dessert, but these take the place of the sweet rolls, croissants, or other sweet breads that are often served.

Oil for frying

12   *small (snack size) flour tortillas*

4   *tart apples (such as pippin), peeled, cored, and cut into ¼-inch wedges*

¼   *cup (½ stick) butter*

   Sugar to taste

10   *ounces cheddar cheese, grated*

   Cinnamon

To Garnish:

1½   *cups sour cream*

   Long strips of rind from 2 firm lemons (use a zester)

Heat about 2 inches of oil in a deep saucepan or wok until hot but not smoking. Fry tortillas one at a time until puffed and lightly browned. Drain on paper towels.

Sauté apple slices in butter in a large skillet over medium heat, stirring often, until slightly softened. Stir in sugar and cook over low heat, stirring often, until apples are crisp-tender. Set aside.

Preheat broiler. Spread about 1 tablespoon shredded Cheddar over each tortilla almost to the edge. Arrange on a baking sheet and slide under hot broiler just long enough to melt the cheese. Set aside.

Mound apple slices in the center of each tostada. Sprinkle with cinnamon and top with sour cream. Garnish each serving with long strips of lemon rind.

To prepare in advance: Fry the tortillas and top with cheese up to 2 hours ahead. Cover with a clean towel and leave at room temperature. Heat and assemble just before serving.

High-Tech Dinner for 2

Baked Artichokes with Goat Cheese Soufflé

Microwave Steamed Trout with Lemon and Mushrooms

Chardonnay or *Fumé Blanc*

Baby Butter Potatoes with Fresh Dill

Blueberry Baked Apples

L.A. has long been attracted by the entertainment and convenience of culinary high-tech, from coffeepots that grind the beans and brew fresh coffee just in time to greet you in the morning to television monitors for viewing video cooking classes right in the kitchen. One of the newest additions is the combination convection-microwave oven.

This menu demonstrates the best features of both oven types – the quick and even baking of the convection oven, and the amazing speed and versatility of the microwave. The first course, huge California artichokes filled with a goat cheese soufflé, puff even higher in a convection oven than in conventional gas or electric models. While the artichokes are on the table, two trout in individual serving dishes are steamed in the microwave for the main course. A dessert of baked apples, which used to require an hour in the oven, is microwave-cooked in moments.

This whole meal can be prepared from start to finish in an hour. For those who wish a more leisurely timetable, parts of it may be prepared the day before and finished within 30 minutes while you and your companion enjoy a glass of chilled Chardonnay.

Timetable

All preparation may be done within 1 hour. The following suggestions are for those who wish a more leisurely preparation.

One day ahead:

Cook artichokes, remove chokes, and chill.

An hour or two before serving:

Make soufflé base.

Prepare trout for microwave oven.

Bake apples.

Twenty-five minutes before serving:

Beat egg whites and fold into soufflé base; fill artichokes and bake.

Just before serving artichokes:

Cook trout.

Cook potatoes.

Baked Artichokes with Goat Cheese Soufflé 2 servings

The soufflé remains somewhat creamy in the center, so it is more saucelike than solid.

2   *large artichokes*

1   *medium onion, sliced*

½   *lemon*

1   *garlic clove, peeled*

2   *tablespoons olive oil*

1   *tablespoon fresh breadcrumbs*

Goat cheese soufflé

1   *tablespoon butter*

1   *medium shallot, minced*

1   *garlic clove, pressed or minced*

1½   *tablespoons all-purpose flour*

3   *tablespoons dry vermouth* or *dry white wine*

⅓   *cup milk* or *light cream (half and half)*

3   *ounces fresh goat cheese (such as Montrachet)*

2   *teaspoons snipped fresh chives*

½   *teaspoon coarse salt*

Several gratings of fresh nutmeg

Pinch of cayenne pepper

2   *eggs, separated*

⅛   *teaspoon cream of tartar*

Paprika

Rinse the artichokes well and trim away the sharp leaf tips. Place several quarts of water in a large stainless steel or enamel pot and add sliced onion, lemon half, garlic clove, and 1 tablespoon olive oil. Bring to boil, add artichokes, and simmer for about 30 minutes, or until barely tender when the hearts are pierced with a fork. Let cool slightly and, without opening them too much, pull out the center leaves to expose the hairy chokes. Using a spoon, scrape away the chokes to expose the hearts. Sprinkle the inside of each prepared artichoke with ½ tablespoon breadcrumbs.

Preheat the oven to 350°F. Brush the remaining 1 tablespoon olive oil over the outsides of the prepared artichokes to keep them from drying out during baking. Place them on a foil-lined baking sheet.

For soufflé, melt the butter in a medium skillet (preferably nonstick) and sauté the shallot and garlic over low heat, taking care not to burn them. Sprinkle flour over the mixture and stir for several minutes. Remove from heat and add the wine and milk or cream. Return to low heat and whisk until smooth and thickened. Add the goat cheese, chives, salt, nutmeg, and cayenne, whisking until smooth. Remove from heat and whisk in the egg yolks one at a time. (If preparing this ahead of time, press plastic wrap into the surface to prevent a skin from forming and set aside for up to 3 hours.)

In a grease-free mixing bowl, whisk the egg whites with the cream of tartar just to the point where they do not slide when the bowl is tilted (soft peaks). Fold half the beaten whites into the goat cheese mixture to lighten it. Pour this mixture over the remaining whites and fold gently but thoroughly.

Spoon the soufflé mixture into the hollows in the prepared artichokes. Sprinkle the top of each lightly with paprika. Bake for 20 minutes, or until the soufflé is set and the top is browned. Serve right away.

To prepare in advance: The artichokes may be prepared the day before. Refrigerate them, covered, then steam briefly to warm them before filling with soufflé. The soufflé base, without beaten egg whites, may be prepared up to 3 hours ahead; leave at room temperature, with plastic wrap pressed into the surface to prevent a skin from forming. Beat the whites and proceed with the recipe just before baking.

Microwave Steamed Trout with Lemon and Mushrooms 2 servings

This is a simple, low-calorie method of cooking trout in individual serving dishes.

2   *fresh whole trout, 12 to 16 ounces each*

3   *whole lemons*

16   *medium mushrooms, cleaned and sliced*

2   *tablespoons minced fresh parsley* or *chervil*

Rinse trout well and blot dry. Place in an ovenproof oval serving dish. Cut one of the lemons in half and squeeze the juice of one half into the cavities of the trout. Use the mushrooms to fill the cavities of the trout. Slice the remaining lemons into six slices each, placing three atop the mushrooms in each cavity. Arrange the remaining lemon slices over the trout, three slices each. Arrange any remaining mushrooms around the trout in the baking dishes. Sprinkle with minced parsley or chervil.

Cover each dish with plastic wrap and use the tip of a knife to pierce two holes in the wrap to let steam escape. Microwave at high power for 10 minutes. Let stand for 5 minutes without removing the plastic wrap, then serve at once. (Trout, being a freshwater fish, must be fully cooked. Check by looking at the flesh next to the backbone; it should be white. If necessary, recover with plastic wrap and cook 1 to 2 minutes longer, letting the fish stand for 3 minutes or so again before serving.)

To bone trout, cut off tail fin and head. Lightly run a knife tip along the stripe that runs the length of the fish, touching the bone beneath as you go. Scrape the skin and flesh below the cut toward you. Scrape the skin and flesh above the cut away from you, revealing the skeleton structure. Cut along backbone to loosen it. At the tail end, lift the skeleton and pull it away from the fish.

Baby Butter Potatoes with Fresh Dill 2 servings

Butter potatoes (sometimes called Finnish or Butterburst potatoes) are all-purpose potatoes with pale golden flesh and a slight butter flavor. Tiny ones are now widely available in Southern California, but small red or white potatoes may be substituted.

1   *pound small yellow potatoes*

1   *tablespoon butter*

2   *teaspoons chopped fresh dill* (or *rosemary* or *tarragon*)

Salt and freshly ground black pepper to taste

Boil the potatoes in water to cover for 10 to 15 minutes, or until tender when pierced with the tip of a sharp knife. Drain and return to the dry saucepan in which they cooked, toss the butter and dill, and season to taste with salt and black pepper.

Blueberry Baked Apples 2 servings

A quick and very low-cal snack or dessert. The blue-berries, combined with spices and the apple's natural juices, create a lovely plum-colored sauce. We enjoy these served warm, with or without cream.

2   *tart green apples, such as Pippin or Granny Smith, cored and peeled halfway from the top of the apple to the bottom*

2   *teaspoons firmly packed brown sugar*

Generous pinch each of cinnamon and freshly grated nutmeg

1   *cup fresh blueberries*

½   *cup crème fraîche, or sweetened whipped cream (optional garnish)*

Place each apple in an individual bowl or other serving dish (make sure the dish has no metallic decoration that would deflect the microwaves). Sprinkle with the brown sugar, spices, and blueberries, allowing some of the berries to slip down into the hole left by removing the core. Cover each tightly with plastic wrap and pierce two holes to let steam escape. Micro-wave one apple at a time at high power for 4 minutes; remove from oven and let stand 5 minutes while you bake the other apple. Remove plastic wrap after 5 minutes. Serve warm.

To prepare in advance: Bake these an hour or so before serving. They will stay warm until time for dessert.

A California Cuisine Dinner for 6 to 8

Pizza with Eggplant, Sun-Dried Tomatoes,
Feta, and Mint

Fumé Blanc

Chicken Breasts in Garlic Parmesan Cream
on a bed of Fresh Zucchini and Carrot Pasta

Gremolata Garnish

Chardonnay, Cabernet Sauvignon or Zinfandel

Carrot Flowers with Green Bean Stems

Hot Apricot Soufflé

This menu, exemplifying the freshness of California cuisine, is amazingly quick to prepare – especially if pizza dough has been made ahead and frozen, and if the carrot flowers have been carved the night before.

Pizza has become an any-time-of-day snack, and here we have topped our favorite crust with an unusual assortment of toppings to serve as a savory appetizer, cut into wedges or squares.

The chicken is especially tender after being "velvetized" with a cornstarch coating in the Chinese manner before cooking. The creamy, garlicky sauce, spiked with Parmesan, makes the chicken special enough to serve on its own, or on pasta laced with thin strips of fresh vegetables.

The plate garnish for the main course was inspired by a dinner at one of our favorite L.A. restaurants, St. Estéphe, where Chef John Sedlar once served us a plate decorated with a bouquet of carrot flowers with stems made from tiny *haricots verts* and leaves of zucchini. Paul's version, which is much simpler for the home chef, uses fresh green beans that have been "frenched" into long, thin strips for use when the tiny beans are not available in our local markets.

Dessert, a marvelous puff of apricot-flavored meringue, just may be the speediest soufflé ever created.

Timetable

A week or more ahead:

Make and freeze pizza dough.

Make and freeze pasta.

One to 2 days ahead:

Prepare gremolata; cover with damp paper towel; refrigerate.

Cut carrot flowers for garnish.

Up to 8 hours ahead:

Make soufflé base.

An hour before guests arrive:

Assemble and bake pizza.

Cook chicken and keep warm; keep sauce separate.

Blanch green beans for garnish.

After guests arrive:

Cook pasta; toss with carrots and zucchini.

Beat egg whites, fold into soufflé base; bake.

Soften ice cream for soufflé sauce.

Pizza with Eggplant, Sun-Dried Tomatoes, Feta, and Mint 8 servings

Pizza is a dish we've learned to fix at home very quickly. Here we were inspired by some ingredients we had on hand, including fresh mint from our garden, to create an appetizer with a Mediterranean flavor.

1 *recipe Basic Pizza Crust (page 14)*

Topping:

3 *small Japanese eggplants (or 1 medium eggplant, sliced ½ inch thick, then cut into 1-inch squares)*

Salt

Olive oil

8 *to 12 sun-dried tomatoes, and a bit of oil from their jar (see Note)*

2   thin slices red onion, separated into rings

2   to 3 tablespoons chopped fresh mint

4   ounces feta cheese or fresh goat cheese, crumbled

8   ounces (2 cups) shredded part-skim mozzarella cheese

Note: Sun-dried tomatoes, packed in olive oil and flavored with garlic and herbs, are available in jars in gourmet specialty stores. They are expensive, but a little goes a long way to lend a piquant flavor to many salads, pizzas, and pasta dishes.

Prepare basic pizza dough as directed in the recipe. Place rack in bottom third of oven and preheat to 425°F for 30 minutes before baking.

To make the topping, cut the eggplant diagonally into ½-inch-thick slices, sprinkle with salt, and arrange slices on a platter or cutting board. Top with a plate, then with a weight (such as heavy cans) to press out the excess liquid. Let drain for 30 minutes, rinse with cold water, and blot dry. Brush the eggplant with olive oil and arrange on baking sheet. Bake for about 15 to 20 minutes, or until browned on both sides, turning once. Remove eggplant, leaving oven lit.

Arrange the eggplant, sun-dried tomatoes, onion, mint, feta, and shredded mozzarella evenly over the surface of the pizza to within 1 inch of the edge. Drizzle a tablespoon or so of the oil from the tomato jar over the surface of the pizza. Bake for 20 minutes, or until the crust is browned and crisp. Let rest at room temperature for 5 minutes before serving.

To prepare in advance: Pizza can be baked ahead of time, then reheated at 425°F for 10 minutes or so, until hot.

Chicken Breasts in Garlic Parmesan Cream 8 servings

Gremolata, a colorful combination of citrus peels, garlic, and parsley, adds sparkle to this dish. It adds a lot of flavor and color and no calories, so we keep it on hand as a garnish for many dishes from salads to stews.

4   *whole chicken breasts, split, boned, and skinned*

   Coarse salt

   Cornstarch, to coat chicken

3   *tablespoons butter*

3   *tablespoons vegetable oil*

2   *garlic cloves, minced or pressed*

½   *cup dry vermouth* or ⅔ *cup dry white wine*

1½   *cups heavy cream*

½   *cup freshly grated Parmesan cheese*

2   *teaspoons fresh lemon juice, or to taste*

   Cayenne pepper

Gremolata:

2   *garlic cloves, minced*

¼   *cup minced fresh parsley*

2   *teaspoons minced orange rind*

2   *teaspoons minced lemon rind*

Garnish:

Carrot flowers with green bean stems
(directions follow)

Cut the chicken breasts in half crosswise to make 16 pieces. Place between sheets of waxed paper and pound lightly with the bottom of a skillet to flatten

slightly. Sprinkle with salt and dredge in cornstarch. Set aside for 10 to 20 minutes, during which time the cornstarch will tenderize the chicken and make it especially succulent.

Melt the butter with the oil in a heavy large skillet. (If necessary, cook the chicken in two batches, or use two skillets.) Sauté the chicken pieces over medium-high heat until brown on one side, then turn to brown the other side. Reduce the heat to low, cover, and cook for 5 to 7 minutes, or until just cooked through. Remove from the skillet to a warm platter. Pour off the drippings, leaving any crusty brown bits in the pan.

Over medium heat sauté the garlic briefly, without allowing it to color, then add the wine and boil until almost evaporated. Add the cream and cook, stirring from time to time, until the consistency of a sauce. Reduce the heat to its lowest setting. Whisk in the Parmesan and heat gently just until melted. Remove sauce from the heat and season with lemon juice and cayenne to taste; do not heat after adding lemon juice.

For gremolata, simply combine all the ingredients and set aside.

To serve, pour off any juices from the reserved chicken pieces. Spoon sauce over pasta (see next recipe) and top each serving with two pieces of chicken. Sprinkle with gremolata.
To prepare in advance: The entire dish, except gremolata, may be reheated in its serving dish in a low oven, though it is likely that juices from the chicken will thin the sauce. Top with gremolata just before serving.

Carrot Flowers with Green Bean Stems for 8 plate garnishes

This fresh and colorful plate garnish is beautiful and edible. It can be used with any simple meat, fish, or poultry course.

3   *medium carrots, peeled*

1   *pound young, slender green beans*

Using a sharp paring knife, make four diagonal cuts in the small end of one carrot, forming four sides (see figure 1). Using the very tip of the knife, and starting just a little higher up on the carrot, cut just behind each of the previous cuts to form petals. Gently twist (see figure 2) the flower off the end of the carrot. Repeat until you have 24 flowers. (Mistakes are edible.)

"French" the green beans using a sharp knife or a gadget made especially for that purpose (see figure 3).

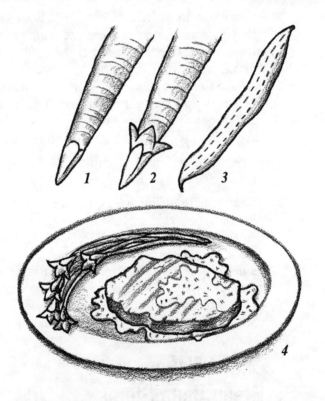

Before serving, steam the carrot flowers and the green beans, separately, until just tender. Arrange a small handful of beans on the plate and decorate with three carrot flowers (see figure 4).

Fresh Pasta with Strips of Zucchini and Carrot 8 servings

All kinds of fresh pasta can now be purchased conveniently in gourmet delis, pasta shops, and even supermarkets. Nevertheless, we often make our own and ask guests to join in, using either an electric pasta maker or a hand-cranked pasta roller. No directions are necessary for the electric machine, but the following is our method for making pasta by hand or with a rolling machine.

2 *cups unbleached all-purpose flour*

1 *cup semolina (see Note)*

3 *large eggs*

1 *tablespoon olive oil*

1 *teaspoon salt*

2 *or more tablespoons lukewarm water*

1 *small zucchini*

1 *carrot*

2 *tablespoons salt*

1 *tablespoon olive oil*

1 *tablespoon butter*

Note: Semolina is made from the hard, coarse endosperm portion of durum wheat. It is an amber-colored, granular flour available in fine or medium grinds in Italian, Middle Eastern and East Indian markets, and in health food stores. The finest grind is the preferred flour to use in making fresh pasta because it requires less kneading than coarser grinds. If semolina is not available, use all-purpose flour for the entire amount.

Combine the flour, semolina, eggs, olive oil, salt, and 2 tablespoons water in a food processor fitted with the steel blade and process to a ball, or mix by hand in the following manner: Mix the flour and semolina on a work surface or in a bowl and make a well in the center. Drop in the eggs, olive oil, and salt. Mix with your fingers or a fork until crumbly. Sprinkle in the warm water 1 tablespoon at a time, while you mix, press, and knead the dough until it can be gathered into a ball. Add more water only if you cannot gather the dough into a ball; the dough should not be sticky. If it is, work in a little more flour until no longer sticky.

Divide the dough into four balls and place each one in a plastic bag or under plastic wrap to keep them from drying out as you work.

Hand method: Knead the dough by hand until smooth and elastic, then roll it out on a floured surface with a long rolling pin until very thin; keep it lightly floured to prevent sticking. Roll it up tightly and cut crosswise into ribbons of the desired width.

Manual pasta machine: It is a good deal easier to knead and roll out the pasta in a manually cranked pasta machine. Set the rollers as far apart as possible. Flatten one piece of dough with your palm into a ¼- to ⅓-inch thick rectangle and flour it lightly. Feed the rectangle through the rollers of the machine; it will emerge as a ragged sheet. Fold the sheet in half crosswise, flour lightly, and run it through the rollers again. Repeat this folding, flouring, and rolling process about 8 times, or until the dough is very smooth and elastic. Lightly flour the sheet of dough and lay it on a strip of waxed paper or a kitchen towel to rest while you work the remaining portions of dough. When all the sheets are rolled, set the rollers a notch closer and feed the first piece of dough through again. Reroll each piece of dough 4 or 5 more times, folding, dusting lightly with flour if sticky, and moving the rollers closer with each rolling. Finish by putting the dough through the machine until the sheets

are the proper thickness (about $\frac{1}{16}$ inch). Machines vary, so you may have to experiment a bit.

Let the sheets of pasta dry for 10 minutes before running through the cutting rollers. For linguine or tagliarini, which are best for this recipe, use the finest cutters on the machine. As you cut the noodles, hand them from a rack or broom handle or lay them in a single layer on a towel. Pasta should dry for at least 15 minutes before it is cooked.

Cut the zucchini and carrot into very fine lengthwise strips using a citrus zester or a long, thin, very sharp knife. These strips should be so fine that they require no cooking, only tossing with the hot cooked pasta.

Cook the pasta in at least 6 quarts of boiling water, adding 2 tablespoons salt and 1 tablespoon olive oil. When water is boiling rapidly, drop in the pasta by handfuls. Homemade pasta cooks very quickly, usually in 20 to 30 seconds, so watch it carefully. Drain immediately in a colander. It is not necessary to rinse pasta if you have used sufficient water, but you can rinse it with boiling water if you wish. Drain well. Return it to the dry cooking pot and toss with butter and the fine strips of zucchini and carrot. Serve immediately.

To prepare in advance: Fresh pasta, after its brief drying period, may be stored in plastic bags in the refrigerator for up to 48 hours, or frozen for up to a month. Or, it may be dried *completely* and stored in an airtight container at room temperature. If frozen, do not thaw before cooking.

Hot Apricot Soufflé 8 servings

This easy soufflé can be made from scratch in 20 minutes! The top of the soufflé has the taste and appearance of a roasted marshmallow.

Butter and sugar for soufflé dish

12   *ounces apricot preserves*

2   *tablespoons Myers's dark rum or Grand Marnier*

1   *tablespoon fresh lemon juice*

   Grated rind of 1 orange

   Pinch of salt

8   *egg whites, at room temperature*

¼   *teaspoon cream of tartar or ½ teaspoon fresh lemon juice (for beating whites)*

1   *tablespoon superfine sugar*

1   *pint French vanilla ice cream*

   Confectioners sugar

Butter the inside of a 7-cup soufflé dish and dust with sugar. Set rack in lower third of oven and preheat to 400°F.

In a very large mixing bowl combine the apricot preserves, rum, 1 tablespoon lemon juice, grated rind, and salt. In a large, grease-free bowl, whisk the whites with cream of tartar until they form soft peaks. Whisk in the superfine sugar and beat a few seconds longer.

Using a large rubber spatula, fold ¼ of the beaten whites into the apricot mixture to lighten it, then fold in the remaining whites. Turn the mixture into the prepared dish. Gently smooth the top and run the spatula vertically around the top of the soufflé, about 1 inch in from the edge, to form a trench (this will give the soufflé a "high hat"). Bake until browned and puffed, about 10 to 12 minutes.

Meanwhile, soften ice cream by beating with a wooden spoon. (For best consistency, do not melt it completely.)

Sift confectioners sugar over the top of the soufflé while it is still on the oven rack. Serve immediately with ice cream sauce.

To prepare in advance: This soufflé holds much better than most. Leave it in the turned-off oven for 10 minutes or a bit longer.

Dinner for 6 at Sheila and Michael Ricci's

Zucchini Madeleines

*Garden Salad with Fresh Corn and
Balsamic Vinegar Dressing*

*Stuffed Leg of Lamb with Sherried Brown
Sauce and Wild Mushrooms*

Cabernet Sauvignon or Pinot Noir

Roasted Yellow, Red, and Green Peppers

Irish Oatmeal Bread

English Manor House Pie with Two Creams

Sheila Ricci is a delightful Englishwoman and a friend of long standing who has a passion for food, her family, and living the good life. She has pursued her interest in cooking in many of the world's finest kitchens, including Chez Panisse, where she was an assistant chef to Alice Waters, and with Gérard Besson in Paris. She was "tea mistress" at Trumps Restaurant in Los Angeles, probably the most stylish place in town for an afternoon meeting.

The Mediterranean-style home she shares with her husband Michael is a kaleidoscope of an environment, for Sheila is a very visual person and a collector of modern paintings and furniture. An evening there recently began with Champagne and freshly baked Zucchini Madeleines in the living room (this year, Milan modern), where we were seated on Mackintosh chairs and watched a video of Pavarotti at Royal Albert Hall on the occasion of the Queen Mother's 81st birthday.

The dining room is actually part of the artfully designed Mediterranean kitchen, so that Sheila can chat with her guests and not miss any of the conversation while she prepares the colorful courses of her menu. She is one of the few friends we have who cook for us, and we appreciate the experience all the more because we are able to watch her work. Her cooking exemplifies the use of classic British and European techniques combined with a deep appreciation of the finest available local ingredients. So in love is she with baby lettuces that she plants and carefully tends a patio garden that provides enough leaves for garden-fresh salads nearly year-round.

She is a staunch believer that every dish should be at the height of freshness and that *nothing* should be in the freezer except ice cubes and any linens waiting to be ironed! We hope she will overlook the directions we've included for preparing a few of her recipes in advance.

Sheila has her own standards of excellence and she settles for nothing less, as you will see in this menu.

Timetable

A week or more ahead:

Bake and freeze madeleines, if desired.

Prepare concentrated veal stock; freeze.

One to 2 days ahead:

Bone and stuff leg of lamb.

Roast and peel peppers; chill

Up to 8 hours ahead:

Thaw madeleines and veal stock.

Prepare salad greens in bowl, cover with damp paper towels, and chill.

Marinate corn in salad dressing.

Assemble pie for baking.

An hour before guests arrive:

Prepare zucchini madeleines if not frozen in advance.

Place lamb in oven.

Bring peppers to room temperature.

Bake pie.

After guests arrive:

Reheat madeleines, if needed.

Finish sauce for lamb.

Cook mushrooms.

Zucchini Madeleines makes 4 dozen or more

The traditional madeleine is a small French cake baked in a special pan with shell-shaped indentations. Sheila serves her savory variation warm, in a napkin-lined basket.

Butter and flour for the madeleine pans

6 *medium zucchini, shredded (5 cups)*

1 *teaspoon salt*

1 *cup all-purpose flour*

1 *cup freshly grated Parmesan cheese (about 5 ounces)*

1½ *teaspoons baking powder*

¾ *teaspoon freshly ground black pepper*

1 *medium onion, minced*

1 *small garlic clove, minced*

5 *eggs, well beaten*

6 *tablespoons (¾ stick) butter, melted*

¼ *cup olive oil*

Set rack in center of oven and preheat to 350°F. Butter madeleine pans generously and dust with flour.

Sprinkle zucchini with salt, let stand 30 minutes, then place in a clean towel and squeeze out excess moisture.

In a mixing bowl combine the flour, Parmesan, baking powder, and pepper. In another bowl, mix together the zucchini, onion, garlic, eggs, melted butter, and oil. Pour this mixture into the dry ingredients and stir until well combined.

Spoon batter into the indentations in the prepared pans, filling them almost full, and smooth the surface. Bake until puffed and browned, 20 to 25 minutes. Serve warm.

To prepare in advance: Sheila doesn't believe in freezing anything, but we've had great success at freezing these, thawing them, and reheating at 350°F for 5 to 10 minutes, or until heated through.

Garden Salad with Fresh Corn and Balsamic Vinegar Dressing 6 servings

Sheila grows baby lettuce in her patio garden, each patch covered by a dome of wire screening to protect it from the abundant small wildlife that surrounds her house. Fortunately for those of us not so gifted with such patience and gardening expertise, many of these greens are available now at farmer's markets and supermarkets.

An Assortment of the Following Greens, to Equal 4 to 5 Cups:

Baby romaine lettuce (2 inches long)

Arugula (3 to 4 inches long)

Mustard cress (2 inches long)

Oak leaf lettuce (1 inch long)

Baby spinach (center, very tender leaves only), stems removed

Dressing:

2   to 3 teaspoons balsamic vinegar

2   sun-dried tomatoes packed in olive oil (see Note), drained and cut into fine julienne

½   cup light olive oil

1   ear fresh corn

2   to 3 leaves fresh basil, minced

Note: Sun-dried tomatoes are available packed in olive oil at gourmet specialty shops. Do not use the dry-pack type for this recipe.

Gently wash the greens and dry thoroughly. Place them in a salad bowl.

For dressing, combine the vinegar and sun-dried tomato strips; whisk in the olive oil. Cut corn from the cob (yes, raw – it will have a firm but tender texture, which is excellent in salads) and add the kernels to the dressing along with the basil.

Pour some of the dressing over the greens and toss *very gently* with clean hands, using a light touch.

To prepare in advance: The corn may marinate in the dressing at room temperature for several hours. Toss with greens just before serving.

Stuffed Leg of Lamb with Sherried Brown Sauce and Wild Mushrooms 10 servings

Veal stock reductions are used a great deal in Los Angeles restaurants to create very simple sauces. Here Sheila combines that idea with a British favorite, leg of lamb, and some locally grown Japanese forest mushrooms.

1   *leg of lamb, 5 to 6 pounds (Sheila prefers the flavor of American or English lamb to that of New Zealand lamb)*

Stuffing:

½   *cup fresh breadcrumbs*

    Leaves of 1 sprig fresh tarragon, chopped

1   *to 2 shallots, minced*

    Salt and freshly ground white pepper

Sauce:

2   *tablespoons (¼ stick) butter*

12	to 16 ounces fresh shiitake, oyster, or other wild mushrooms, as available
1½	cups concentrated brown stock (recipe follows)
2	tablespoons Sherry or Madeira
1	tablespoon reserved lamb drippings, thoroughly degreased

Preheat oven to 500°F for 30 minutes before roasting lamb.

Bone the lamb by making an incision along the side of the roast toward the bone and cutting around the bone (or have the butcher do this for you). Open the meat up, fat side down. Use a small, very sharp knife to trim any very thick parts so that the meat will cook evenly, placing the trimmings over the thin parts.

For stuffing, combine the stuffing ingredients and spread in the center of the meat. Fold the meat over to enclose the stuffing. Use string to tie securely lengthwise, and then at 3-inch intervals crosswise to form a neat roll.

Place on a rack in a roasting pan and roast for 20 minutes, then lower the oven temperature to 325°F and continue cooking for 1 hour longer, or until thermometer inserted in the thickest part of the meat reads 145°F.

Transfer the roast to a platter and let rest for at least 10 minutes before carving. Pour the drippings into a measuring cup and spoon all fat from the surface.

For sauce, melt the butter in a large skillet. Add the mushrooms and cook over medium heat for 2 to 3 minutes, or until softened, then add the brown stock and Sherry. Simmer 5 minutes longer, or until syrupy. Add the lamb drippings; taste and correct seasoning.

Spoon sauce (without mushrooms) onto warm serving plates and top with thin crosswise slices of lamb. Garnish with the cooked mushrooms.

To prepare in advance: The lamb may be stuffed and tied the night before cooking *if both meat and stuffing are chilled.* Cook just before serving.

Brown Veal Stock makes 2 quarts

Many modern recipes call for sauces made with reduced homemade stock. It is time-consuming to make, but you just can't buy fine stock in a can; it is essential to make your own. This is a classic veal stock. Beef may be substituted for the veal, but the sauce will have a different flavor and will not contain enough gelatin to give the reduction a glazed consistency.

4   *to 5 pounds veal bones, including some knuckle if possible, sawed into manageable pieces*

3   *onions, coarsely chopped*

2   *carrots, peeled and cut into 1-inch lengths*

1   *large leek*

2   *celery stalks, including leafy tops*

2   *teaspoons salt*

> *Bouquet garni: Tie together in rinsed cheesecloth some parsley stems, 2 garlic cloves, 1 bay leaf, 1 teaspoon dried thyme, 10 black peppercorns, 4 whole cloves*

Place rack in center of oven and preheat to 450°F. Place the bones, onions, and carrots in a roasting pan and roast, basting with drippings from time to time, until quite brown, about 40 minutes. Some of the onions may even blacken, which will lend a rich color to the stock.

Transfer the ingredients to a large stockpot, leaving the fat in the roasting pan. Add all remaining ingredients to the stockpot. Pour off and discard the fat from the roasting pan, leaving behind any brown drippings. Add 1 cup water to the pan and place over direct heat, scraping up browned bits, then pour this deglazing mixture into the stockpot. Add more water to cover the bones and vegetables by 2 inches. Bring to a boil, then simmer rapidly for 10 to 15 minutes, using a spoon to skim off any scum that rises to the surface.

Partially cover the pan and simmer very slowly for at least 5 hours (or better, overnight), during which time the stock will have reduced in volume. Strain out the bones and vegetables. At this point the mixture may be cooled quickly by pouring it into a clean container set in a sink of cold water. Let stand for 20 minutes or so, then skim all fat from the surface. Alternatively, refrigerate overnight, then lift off and discard congealed fat.

Concentrated Brown Stock

Place the brown stock in a clean saucepan and simmer slowly, uncovered, until it is reduced to about 4 cups and is concentrated and syrupy. The time required will depend on the diameter of the pan; a larger diameter pan will allow the sauce to reduce much more rapidly.

To prepare in advance: Refrigerate in a covered container, bringing the stock to a boil every 3 days. It may also be frozen for up to 4 months.

Roasted Yellow, Red, and Green Peppers 6 servings

One of our favorite cooking aromas is that of roasting bell peppers. Yellow ones are now widely available, and we enjoy their special sweetness. If you find some purple peppers, by all means add them to this recipe.

3   *large red bell peppers*

3 large green bell peppers

3 large yellow bell peppers

Roast the peppers directly over a medium-high gas flame on the stove (or broil 1 inch below the broiling element if you have an electric stove), turning them as the skins blacken until they are completely charred all over. Place them in a sealed plastic bag and set aside for 5 minutes.

Remove the peppers from the bag, cut in half lengthwise, and remove stems, seeds, and membranes. Scrape off the charred skin with the dull side of a chef's knife. Rinse briefly and blot dry. Cut peppers lengthwise into strips approximately 2 inches wide and place them on a serving dish.

To Prepare In Advance: Refrigerate, covered, for up to 2 days. Bring to room temperature before serving.

Irish Oatmeal Bread makes 2 loaves

This wonderful coarse loaf is a reflection of Sheila's baking talent, and her appreciation of homemade goodness.

1   *cup boiling water*

1   *cup milk*

1½   *cups Irish oatmeal (see Note)*

¼   *cup treacle (see Note)*

3   *tablespoons unsalted butter*

2   *eggs*

1   *teaspoon salt*

2   *packages active dry yeast*

½   *cup warm water (105 to 115°F)*

5½   *to 6 cups bread flour*

1   *egg yolk beaten with 1 tablespoon water*

Note: These imported ingredients are available at gourmet specialty shops and by mail order through the Williams-Sonoma catalogue. If Irish oatmeal is not available, substitute regular rolled oats (not the "quick cooking" type). Treacle, a syrup similar to molasses but neither as dark nor as thick, is a popular British ingredient, and is sold under the brand name of Tate and Lyle. If not available, substitute light molasses.

Pour boiling water and milk over 1⅓ cups of the oats, reserving the remainder of the oats for sprinkling over the loaves. Add treacle, butter, eggs, and salt. Let stand 30 minutes.

In a small bowl, stir yeast into the ½ cup warm water and let stand 5 minutes; add to the oat mixture. Beat in flour 1 cup at a time. Turn out onto floured board, cover, and let stand 15 minutes.

Knead dough for 10 minutes, or until smooth and satiny, adding flour if needed. Place in a greased bowl, cover, and let rise until doubled, about 2 hours.

Punch dough down and knead briefly. Shape into 2 round loaves. Place on a greased baking sheet. Brush with egg mixture and sprinkle with reserved oats.

Bake for 45 to 50 minutes, or until browned.

To Prepare In Advance: The loaves are best freshly baked and still warm. They may be frozen for up to 3 months.

English Manor House Pie with Two Creams 10 or more servings

Sheila uses an earthenware English pie dish about 12 inches in diameter and 3 inches deep. Lacking such a dish, we have used a variety of oval casseroles of 6-cup capacity with great success. All sorts of imported creams are now found in the gourmet sec-

tion of supermarkets, as well as in specialty shops and cheese stores.

8   *Granny Smith apples, peeled, cored, and cut into 1/4-inch slices*

6   *medium-size firm Damson plums, pitted and quartered (see Note 1)*

1/4 *cup water*

Juice and grated rind of 1 lemon

1/2 *cup sugar*

1   *egg beaten with 1 tablespoon water*

1   *to 2 tablespoons Demerara or turbinado sugar*

Sweet Pie Dough (pâte brisée fine):

1 1/4 *cups all-purpose flour*

1/8 *teaspoon salt*

1/2 *cup (1 stick) unsalted butter*

Two Creams *(see Note 2):*

16   *ounces St. Ival single cream*

16   *ounces yellow double clotted cream with a bit of sugar added to taste, if needed*

Note 1: If Damson plums are not in season, use whatever purple-skinned plums are available; they lend a lovely pink color to the filling. If no plums are available at all, use extra apples (Sheila chops the extra apples finely and mixes them with the slices, creating a lovely sauce consistency after baking).

Note 2: These imported English creams may be difficult to find. Substitute 32 ounces of one kind, Devon cream, crème fraîche, or even good old American whipped cream if desired.

Set rack in center of oven and preheat to 350°F.

Combine apples and plums in a saucepan with

¼ cup cold water. Bring to boil and remove from heat. Transfer to shallow 6-cup earthenware dish. Pour the lemon juice over the fruit and sprinkle with lemon rind and ½ cup sugar.

For dough, prepare pastry by usual method, either by hand or in a food processor. Roll out to fit the top of the baking dish, allowing a 1-inch overhang. Place the pastry over the fruit and flute the edges, securing them to the side of the dish. Brush pastry with egg mixture. Make a few slashes to allow steam to escape. Sprinkle generously with Demerara or turbinado sugar.

Bake for 40 to 60 minutes, or until the crust is nicely browned.

Serve pie warm with both types of cream.

To Prepare In Advance: Sheila serves this only when fresh from the oven and still warm. Leftover pie may be stored, covered, at room temperature for up to 2 days.

Kay Okrand's Menu for a Summer Buffet for 20

Choice of:

Cinzano and soda with slice of lemon

Lillet with orange slice

White wine spritzers

Basket of Raw and Al Dente Vegetables with Sun-Dried Tomato and Basil Mayonnaise

Chicken Piccata

Chardonnay or Fumé Blanc

Stir-Fried Vegetables in Fresh Herb Butter

Pasta Primavera Salad

Five-Leaf Salad

Focaccia with Fresh Rosemary

Amaretto Chiffon Cheesecake in a Macaroon Crust

Long-stemmed Strawberries Dipped in White and Dark Chocolates

Espresso and Cappuccino

Now and then we want a meal to be a real event, but have no time to do all the work ourselves. Time to call in a caterer!

Kay Okrand is one we can trust to prepare and serve a meal in our home just as we would. She prepared this theme menu, which reflects the new style of Italian cooking *(la nuova cucina)*, for 20 guests at an indoor-outdoor party. All the dishes were cooked within an hour of serving and kept warm in chafing dishes. Fresh herbs were very much in evidence, both as flavorings and as attractive garnishes.

Baskets of varying sizes contained imaginative arrangements of raw vegetables for dipping into a mayonnaise flavored with basil and sun-dried tomatoes. A bartender was present to mix the aperitifs.

The main-course buffet presents a bountiful, colorful variety of flavors and textures. Chicken Piccata, a variation of the classic Italian Veal Piccata, consists of boneless chicken breasts sautéed in a tangy lemon-wine sauce and garnished with thin slices of sautéed lemon and a generous sprinkling of capers. The accompanying multi-colored vegetables are stir-fried in butter that has been infused with the fragrance of fresh oregano and thyme leaves, then clarified to prevent burning during the quick cooking. Two very different salads make beautiful displays. One, featuring *fusilli* (spiral) pasta, is studded with broccoli, Mediterranean olives, mushrooms, artichoke hearts, red peppers, and pine nuts. The other, a delicate combination of five kinds of colorful leaves, complements almost any meal, and we serve it with many a company dinner at our house. Kay also likes to serve whatever fresh fruit is available in a large watermelon boat garnished with fresh mint.

When Kay caters a party she often takes advantage of her favorite bakeries. From II Fornaio in Beverly Hills she purchases rosemary bread to serve with sweet butter flavored with Gorgonzola; from La Conversation in the Loz Feliz district come chocolate-dipped macadamia heart cookies and individual lemon tarts. In this menu we have replaced those items with our own recipes for focaccia, a pizza-type bread flavored with fresh rosemary, and amaretto chiffon cheesecake. Both are perfect counterpoints to the light Italian dishes of this buffet.

Timetable

A week or more ahead:

Prepare pesto for dip.

Make dough for focaccia and freeze.

One or 2 days ahead:

Set up bar.

Prepare dip and vegetables; chill.

Prepare greens for five-leaf salad.

Make cheesecake; chill.

Up to 8 hours ahead:

Slice lemons and oranges for bar.

Prepare herb butter for stir-fried vegetables.

Toss pasta salad; leave at room temperature.

Prepare dressing for five-leaf salad.

Garnish cheesecake (except for flowers).

Dip strawberries in chocolate; chill.

An hour before guests arrive:

Line baskets with kale and arrange vegetables and dip.

Cook chicken and keep warm.

Prepare focaccia for baking; bake if desired.

Place flowers on cheesecake.

After guests arrive:

Stir-fry vegetables.

Bake or reheat focaccia.

Basket of Raw and Al Dente Vegetables with Sun-Dried Tomato and Basil Mayonnaise 20 servings

Two separate baskets of vegetables and mayonnaise dip are set out so that guests do not congregate in one area. For the coffee table in the living room, one large round wicker basket is lined with frilly blue-green leaves of kale, a green that stays crisp for hours at room temperature. Cherry tomatoes, long diagonal cuts of carrot, miniature ears of baby corn from a jar, radishes, cucumber, and jícama spears surround a halved acorn squash holding the dip. A fresh ear of corn, with a strip removed to show the kernels, and half a bright red pepper are decoration. For the patio, kale is used to line a long oval wicker basket, and the vegetables, featuring the same items except for cucumber rounds instead of spears, are arranged in rows. The dip is served spectacularly alongside the basket, nestled in the center of a huge Savoy cabbage.

1   to 2 heads kale, to line vegetable baskets

1   acorn squash or other winter squash, to use as container for serving dip

1   large head Savoy cabbage, to use as container for serving dip

1   ear of fresh corn in its husk

1   red bell pepper

Vegetables:

Bottled miniature ears of corn (about 20 ounces – see Note)

2   baskets cherry tomatoes

2   medium jícama, peeled and cut into spears

6   carrots, peeled and cut into thin diagonal slices

2   bunches radishes

4   medium cucumbers, cut into spears or rounds

Mayonnaise dip:

2   cups mayonnaise, preferably homemade

⅔   cup pesto (purchased, or made from recipe that follows)

6   sun-dried tomatoes, minced

Note: Tiny whole ears of corn are available in jars in gourmet specialty shops and Chinese markets. They look wonderful but usually have a slightly tinny taste, so rinse well in cold water before use. We don't recommend buying them in cans.

Line serving baskets with a border of frilly kale leaves and fill with cut vegetables for dipping.

For mayonnaise dip, combine the ingredients. Spoon into the center of a halved and hollowed acorn squash to nestle in a large basket. To serve dip in a Savoy cabbage, spoon it into a bowl-like indentation cut in the center of the head.

To Prepare In Advance: The dip may be stored in the refrigerator for up to 48 hours before serving. Wrap the cut vegetables in damp white paper towels (the dye used in colored or printed paper towels can be transferred to foods) and refrigerate in plastic bags for up to 24 hours.

Pesto makes 2 cups

One of Italy's outstanding sauces is an uncooked paste of fresh sweet basil, hard grating cheese (such as Parmigiano, Romano, or Sardo), garlic, nuts (pine nuts or walnuts), and the finest olive oil. It is a specialty of Genoa, dating back to the time of Virgil. Commercially made pesto is available in the frozen-foods sections of Italian delis and some supermarkets all year, and it can be excellent. The canned or bottled type, which is not refrigerated, is not recommended because the flavor and color suffer greatly in the canning process. The following recipe is from our book, *The von Welanetz Guide to Ethnic Ingredients* (Tarcher/Houghton Mifflin, 1983). Though traditionally made in a marble mortar, pesto is much more easily prepared in an electric food processor.

2   *cups firmly packed fresh basil leaves (no substitute)*

½   *cup fresh parsley leaves*

½   *cup extra-virgin olive oil*

¼   *cup pine nuts* or *walnuts*

2   *garlic cloves, peeled*

1¼   *teaspoons salt*

¾ cup freshly grated Parmesan cheese (up to half this amount can be Romano, if desired)

Combine the basil, parsley, olive oil, nuts, garlic, and salt in a blender or food processor. Process at high speed, stopping the motor occasionally to scrape down the sides of the container with a rubber spatula. When well blended, add the grated cheese and pulse only a second or two to mix; do not over-blend or you will lose the crumbly texture of the Parmesan.

To Prepare In Advance: Refrigerate pesto for up to a week, or freeze (before the addition of grated cheese) in small jars. To thaw, set jar in warm water, stirring until softened, then proceed as directed.

Chicken Piccata 20 servings

These boneless chicken breasts, each garnished with a lemon slice and sprinkled with capers, are easy to serve at buffet-style parties. The recipe allows 1½ breast halves per person, as some guests will take two and some only one.

¼ cup (½ stick) unsalted butter

¼ cup olive oil

3 small garlic cloves, minced

1 cup dry white wine or dry vermouth

1 cup fresh lemon juice

15 whole chicken breasts, split, boned, and skinned to make 30 pieces (see Note)

1 jar (3¼ to 3½ ounces) capers, drained

1 tablespoon mixed fresh herbs or 1 teaspoon dried herbs (Kay uses oregano, basil, rosemary, and thyme)

1½   teaspoons sesame seed

Salt and coarsely ground black pepper to taste

4   thin-skinned lemons, sliced, to garnish

Note: Remove and freeze the chicken tenderloins and use them for another purpose, such as Asian stir-fry dishes.

Heat 1 tablespoon each of butter and olive oil in a very large skillet or sauté pan. Add 1 clove minced garlic and ¼ cup each of wine and lemon juice, followed by 7 to 8 pieces of chicken. Cook over medium heat for 5 minutes, then sprinkle with about ¼ each of the capers, herbs, and sesame seed, salt, and a generous sprinkling of pepper. Turn chicken over and cook about 5 minutes longer, or until just cooked through. Transfer the chicken pieces to a warm platter or chafing dish. Add 1 sliced lemon to the pan drippings and sauté slices for a minute or so on each side, then place atop each piece of chicken. Continue cooking remaining chicken in the same manner until all is done.

To Prepare In Advance: Cover the chicken pieces with foil and keep warm in a low oven for up to an hour (or keep warm in a covered chafing dish). Leftover chicken can be covered and reheated at 350°F for 20 to 30 minutes, or in a microwave oven just until hot.

Stir-Fried Vegetables in Fresh Herb Butter 20 servings

A bit of Asian influence appears in the cooking method here. Clarified butter that has been infused with the flavor of fresh herbs is used as the cooking oil: It will not burn over high heat as regular butter does.

Herb Butter:

1   *cup (2 sticks) butter*

1   *bunch fresh oregano*

1   *bunch fresh thyme*

Vegetables:

1   *pound (about 100) Chinese snow peas*

4   *red bell peppers, seeds and membranes removed, cut into strips*

4   *yellow bell peppers, seeds and membranes removed, cut into strips*

40   *baby carrots, peeled and halved lengthwise or 10 large carrots, peeled and cut into diagonal slices*

20   *miniature crookneck squash, halved lengthwise, or 3 regular-size crookneck squash, cut into diagonal slices*

20   *miniature zucchini, halved lengthwise, or 3 regular-size zucchini, cut into diagonal slices*

1   *bunch fresh oregano, leaves only*

1   *bunch fresh thyme, leaves only*

½   *cup dry white wine or dry vermouth*

Salt and coarsely ground black pepper to taste

For herb butter, melt butter in saucepan and add chopped fresh herbs. Simmer slowly for 10 minutes, pressing herbs with wooden spoon occasionally to release their flavor and aroma. Let stand 10 minutes. Skim foam from surface and discard. Pour the clear yellow clarified butter into another saucepan, leaving the watery portion and herbs in the bottom. (This may be discarded, or strained and reserved for another use such as a topping for baked potatoes.)

Heat half of the clarified butter in a large wok until very hot. Add a mixture of half the vegetables and fresh herb leaves, adding ¼ cup white wine and seasoning with salt and pepper. Stir-fry just until vege-

tables are crisp-tender, then transfer to a warm serving platter. Cook the remaining vegetables in the same manner.

To prepare in advance: Keep vegetables warm in a chafing dish or a low oven (150°F) for up to 30 minutes.

Pasta Primavera Salad 20 servings

This is a particularly tasty salad that lends itself beautifully to being made ahead of time.

1	*large head broccoli*
2	*cups chicken broth*
1½	*cups olive oil*
¾	*cup tarragon vinegar*
¼	*cup fresh lemon juice*
¼	*cup pesto*
3	*garlic cloves, minced*
1	*tablespoon dry mustard*
20	*mushrooms, cleaned and sliced*
2	*pounds pasta:* fusilli *(small spirals) or* penne *(quills) (see Note)*
10	*baby artichokes, cooked just until tender and cut into quarters, or 1 package (10 ounces) frozen artichokes, cooked and quartered, or 2 jars (6 ounces each) marinated artichoke hearts, drained and quartered*
2	*red bell peppers, roasted, peeled, and cut into julienne strips*
1	*bunch scallions, very thinly sliced (including some of the green tops)*
1	*cup Mediterranean-style olives, halved and pitted*
1	*cup coarsely chopped fresh parsley leaves*

4 *ounces pine nuts, lightly browned in 1 tablespoon each butter and olive oil*

Note: To add color to this salad, Kay uses an assortment of colored pastas — white (egg), orange (carrot), rose-colored (tomato), and green (spinach) varieties — purchased from one of the city's many pasta shops. Any small shape of fine-quality dried pasta (such as De Cecco brand) may be used.

Cut the florets from the broccoli and divide into small clusters (reserve the remaining broccoli for another use). Blanch the broccoli in boiling chicken broth for 1 to 2 minutes and drain immediately. Cool (Reserve the chicken broth for another use as well.)

Combine the olive oil, vinegar, lemon juice, pesto, garlic, and dry mustard. Add the sliced mushrooms and marinate while you make the rest of the salad.

Cook the pasta according to package directions, drain, and rinse in cold water to cool it quickly. Let drain of all excess moisture, then place in a large bowl. Add the remaining salad ingredients, the marinated mushrooms from the dressing, and enough dressing to coat the salad. Reserve remaining dressing, if any, for other uses.

To prepare in advance: Pasta salads are at their best when freshly made and at room temperature. If necessary, refrigerate for up to 24 hours. Bring to room temperature before serving.

Five-Leaf Salad 20 servings

This has become a favorite salad at our house and we serve it often, sometimes with the addition of coarsely chopped walnuts if the menu is less complex than this one.

Raspberry Vinaigrette:

1   *cup olive oil*

½   *cup raspberry vinegar (see Note)*

2   *tablespoons fresh lemon juice*

2   *teaspoons Dijon mustard*

     Salt and coarsely ground black pepper

Salad Ingredients:

2   *heads Boston, butter, or Bibb lettuce*

2   *heads red-leaf lettuce*

1   *head curly endive*

2   *bunches watercress*

2   *heads radicchio*

¾   *cup chopped walnuts (optional)*

Note: Raspberry vinegar is an ancient ingredient that has lately become popular again, and several commercial brands are available. If you plan 3 weeks ahead you may make 1 cup of it yourself by combining 1 basket (1¼ cups) fresh red raspberries, 1 tablespoon sugar, and 1 cup fine-quality red wine vinegar in the top of a glass, ceramic, or stainless steel double boiler. Bring the water in the bottom of the double boiler to a simmer and cook vinegar mixture, uncovered, for 10 minutes. Transfer to a container with a lid and refrigerate for 3 weeks. Strain out berries, pressing on pulp. After straining, vinegar can be stored in the refrigerator indefinitely.

To make the dressing, combine ingredients in a jar and shake. Taste and adjust seasoning.

Wash and thoroughly dry salad greens. Tear into bite-size pieces and place in a salad bowl. Toss with dressing and optional walnuts just before serving.

To prepare in advance: Wash and tear greens and spread in a single layer on clean kitchen towels; roll up and

refrigerate for up to 36 hours. Combine dressing ingredients several hours ahead and leave at room temperature until serving time; shake before pouring.

Focaccia with Fresh Rosemary
makes one 12-inch round loaf
Prepare two loaves for 20 servings

Focaccia is pizza dough baked without elaborate toppings. A version flavored with garlic and fresh herbs is replacing garlic bread in popularity with Southern Californians. Pine-needled rosemary grows abundantly throughout the area, and is often used as an ornamental hedge around homes and condominium complexes.

1 *recipe Basic Pizza Crust (see page 17)*

Topping:

¼ *cup olive oil*

1 *to 2 garlic cloves, minced or pressed*

1 *tablespoon minced fresh rosemary*

 Coarse or kosher salt

¼ *cup (½ stick) butter, melted*

Place rack in bottom third of oven and preheat to 425°F for 30 minutes, with pizza stone or tile if using it.

Prepare pizza dough, but allow 30 to 45 minutes for each rising period. Lightly sprinkle a heavy pizza pan, baking sheet, or wooden "peel" (the paddle used to slide pizza onto hot oven tile) with cornmeal. Press dough into a flat disc, then stretch with hands into a 12-inch circle. Set aside for 30 to 45 minutes.

Combine olive oil, garlic, and rosemary. Spread the mixture over the dough to within ½ inch of the edge. Sprinkle with salt. Bake for approximately 20 minutes,

or until the crust is browned and crisp. Remove from oven and brush with melted butter. Let stand 10 minutes before cutting into wedges for serving.

To prepare in advance: Focaccia is best served hot from the oven, but it can be baked ahead of time, then reheated at 425°F for 10 minutes or until hot.

Amaretto Chiffon Cheesecake in a Macaroon Crust 10 servings
Prepare two cheesecakes for 20 servings

This airy, light cheesecake has a wonderful combination of flavors. We like to decorate it with African violet blooms or nasturtiums; a list of other nontoxic flowers follows the recipe.

12   *(about) double, wrapped amaretti cookies (see Note), to make 1¼ cups crumbs*

¼   *cup (½ stick) unsalted butter, softened*

2   *ounces semisweet or bittersweet chocolate, chopped*

Filling:

1   *pound cream cheese, at room temperature*

½   *cup amaretto liqueur*

1   *envelope unflavored gelatin*

¾   *cup cold water*

3   *eggs, separated*

¾   *cup sugar*

2   *teaspoons finely grated orange rind*

2   *teaspoons finely grated lemon rind*

    Pinch of salt

1   *cup heavy cream*

Garnish:

¾ *cup heavy cream, whipped and sweetened with 3 table-spoons confectioners sugar, to garnish*

Fresh, nontoxic flowers (chart follows)

6 *small fresh mint or citrus leaves*

1 *tablespoon reserved amaretti crumbs*

Note: Amaretti are exceptionally fine, crisp macaroons studded with coarse sugar crystals. They are sold in attractive red and orange cans labeled Amaretti di Saronno, under the brand name Lazzaroni, in Italian markets and gourmet specialty shops. The ones labeled *amaretti* are paper-wrapped in pairs. *Amarettini* are tiny cookies with the same flavor, but without the paper wrapping.

Preheat oven to 350°F. Set aside 1 tablespoon crumbs for garnish. Combine the remaining crumbs (a food processor is ideal for making the crumbs and combin-ing the crust ingredients) and the soft butter. Press onto the bottom of a 9-inch springform pan. Bake for 10 to 12 minutes, or until lightly browned. Remove from the oven and place the chopped chocolate on the hot crust. After a few minutes, spread melted chocolate evenly over the crust. Chill until ready to fill.

For filling, beat the cream cheese in the bowl of an electric mixer until very smooth, scraping the sides of the bowl often with a rubber spatula. Gradually beat in the amaretto. Set aside.

Soften the gelatin by sprinkling it over ¼ cup cold water; let stand for 5 minutes. Beat the yolks lightly in a heavy 2- to 3-quart saucepan. Stir in the remain-ing ½ cup water and ½ cup of the sugar and stir con-stantly over moderate heat just until the mixture coats a spoon. Remove from heat, add softened gelatin mix-ture, and stir until dissolved. Gradually beat the warm yolk mixture into the cream cheese mixture, scraping

the sides of the bowl often. Beat in the orange and lemon rinds. Transfer the mixture to a very large mixing bowl and cool completely to room temperature.

In the clean bowl of an electric mixer, whip the egg whites with the salt until they hold soft peaks (they will not slide when the bowl is tilted). Gradually add the remaining ¼ cup sugar, while beating, to stabilize the whites. Transfer the whites to another mixing bowl. In the same bowl used for the whites, whip the cream until it holds soft peaks.

Gradually fold about ⅓ of the cheese mixture into the whites, then fold all the whites back into the cheese mixture. Gradually fold some of this mixture into the whipped cream, then fold the whipped cream back into the cheese mixture.

Pour the filling over the prepared crust. Refrigerate at least 6 hours.

For garnish, pipe sweetened whipped cream in a circle of rosettes on top the cake next to the edge. Pipe more cream rosettes in the center of the cake and top with violets, nasturtiums, or other nontoxic flowers and mint or citrus leaves. Sprinkle some macaroon crumbs between the outer and inner circles of whipped cream rosettes. Remove the sides of the springform before serving.

To prepare in advance: The cheesecake may be prepared up to 48 hours ahead. It is best to decorate it within 6 hours of serving.

Long-Stemmed Strawberries Dipped in White and Dark Chocolates 20 servings

Chocolate-dipped strawberries are not new, but they are still very popular, and we like Kay's idea of drizzling dark chocolate over those dipped in white chocolate, and vice versa.

48	*large perfect strawberries with stems*
6	*ounces dark dipping chocolate (see Note)*
6	*ounces white chocolate*
	Vegetable oil, if needed

Note: Dipping chocolates may be purchased at gourmet specialty shops, or use 3-ounce bars of imported chocolate sold in the candy section of most supermarkets. We recommend the widely available Tobler Tradition and Lindt Excellence for dark chocolate, and Tobler Narcisse for white.

Make sure the strawberries are clean and very dry. Chop the chocolates coarsely and place each in the top of a double boiler (or in a heatproof bowl). Place over hot, not boiling, water, stirring just until dissolved.

Insert a sturdy toothpick into the top of each strawberry next to the stem. Holding onto the toothpick, dip each strawberry into the chocolate, coating it ¾ of the way to the top; leave the green hull and some red visible for the most decorative effect. Spear the free end of the toothpick into a piece of styrofoam so the strawberries can dry upside down, or rest the strawberries on waxed paper. Continue in this manner, dipping half the strawberries in dark chocolate and half in white.

To decorate, thin the remaining chocolate, if necessary, with a small amount of vegetable oil to a drizzling consistency. Drizzle the contrasting color of chocolate over the coated parts of the dipped strawberries from the tip of a table knife or spoon. Chill briefly to harden.

To prepare in advance: We have successfully kept dipped strawberries chilled for up to 8 hours. They begin to soften inside once they are coated, however, so the sooner they are served after coating the better.

A Quick and Fresh Vegetarian Supper for 6

Belgian Endive with
Hazelnut Mayonnaise Dip

Avocado Pasta with Green Beans
and Fresh Tomato Sauce

Barbera

Black Cherry Sorbet with Dark Rum

or

Fresh Fruit with California Zabaglione

We have many friends who choose not to eat meat for an assortment of reasons. Most of them are lacto-vegetarians, which means they do eat a limited amount of eggs, cheese, and dairy products. With the trend toward lighter eating, many people nowadays choose to enjoy "vegetarian days" one or more times a week.

This particular menu is very quick to prepare, and it lets you involve the guests in preparing the component parts. Homemade pasta, always a special treat, is made especially interesting by a trick we learned from James Beard at a cooking class in Seaside, Oregon. He taught us to use mashed avocado in place of a portion of the eggs and all the oil called for in a traditional pasta recipe. It was love at first bite. By serving equal portions of cooked pasta and freshly cooked green beans, you have the main course of a very light meal.

Two dessert ideas are offered with this menu. One, a sort of sorbet, is made in minutes from solidly frozen black cherries pureed in a food processor with dark rum and grated orange rind. It is very light eating and fits the theme of the menu perfectly. The other, more dramatic, dessert is zabaglione, whipped up in a copper saucepan. Guests always enjoy the excitement of watching it foam up in the pan to be served as a frothy sauce for fresh fruit. Here the zabaglione is flavored with California sparkling wine.

Timetable

One day ahead:

Prepare hazelnut mayonnaise.

Cook sauce for pasta.

Up to 8 hours ahead:

Prepare pasta and freeze.

An hour before guests arrive:

Trim Belgian endive.

Prepare garnish for sorbet.

Place fruit for zabaglione in serving dishes.

After guests arrive:

Steam green beans.

Cook pasta.

Reheat sauce.

Prepare sorbet or zabaglione.

Belgian Endive with Hazelnut Mayonnaise Dip Makes 1 cup

This flavorful mayonnaise can double as a spread for cold chicken or steamed fish.

1   cup mayonnaise, preferably homemade

2   teaspoons hazelnut oil (see Note)

1   teaspoon fresh lemon juice

¼   cup coarsely chopped toasted hazelnuts (filberts)

2   heads Belgian endive

Note: Hazelnut oil or *huile de noisette*, which has the flavor and aroma of roasted hazelnuts, is available in gourmet specialty shops and many supermarkets. Store it in a cool place for up to 6 months, or in the refrigerator if you want to keep it longer, but bring to room temperature to reliquefy before use.

Whisk the mayonnaise in a small mixing bowl while gradually drizzling in the hazelnut oil and lemon juice. Fold in most of the hazelnuts, reserving about 1 tablespoon. Transfer to a small serving bowl and sprinkle reserved hazelnuts over the top as a garnish.

Remove the leaves from the Belgian endive by trimming away the ends of the heads. Arrange the leaves spoke–fashion around the bowl of dip.

To prepare in advance: Hazelnut mayonnaise will keep nicely in a covered container in the refrigerator for up to a week. Prepare the endive just before serving.

Avocado Pasta with Green Beans and Fresh Tomato Sauce 4 to 6 servings

Avocado colors this fresh pasta a pale green and gives it a slightly nutty flavor.

Avocado Pasta:

3   *cups unbleached all-purpose flour* or *other flours of your choice*

½   *ripe avocado, mashed (see Note)*

2   *eggs, lightly beaten*

½   *teaspoon salt*

8   *ounces fresh* haricots verts or *green beans, French-cut if desired*

Fresh Tomato Sauce:

2   *tablespoons (¼ stick) butter or margarine*

2   *tablespoons olive oil*

1   *medium onion, minced*

3   *garlic cloves, minced or pressed*

½   *medium-size green bell pepper, seeded and diced*

1   *strip lemon rind or a thin slice of lemon*

1   *tablespoon chopped fresh basil or 1 teaspoon dried, crumbled*

1   *tablespoon chopped fresh parsley*

4   *cups chopped fresh, ripe tomatoes (it is not necessary to peel them)* or, *if fresh tomatoes are not available, 1 can (28 ounces) crushed tomatoes in tomato puree*

     Salt and freshly ground pepper, if needed

2   *tablespoons salt*

1   *tablespoon vegetable or olive oil*

Note: Avocado makes a delicate, pale green pasta. Other colors of pasta may be made by substituting ½ cup steamed and pureed carrot, spinach or beets for the avocado.

For pasta, prepare according to directions in pasta recipe starting on page 46, substituting the mashed avocado for one of the eggs and the 1 tablespoon olive oil. Let the sheets of pasta dry on a towel for 10 minutes before running through the cutting rollers. For *fettucine* (ribbons), the pasta should be ¼ to ½ inch wide. After cutting the dough as desired, let dry on towels or on a rack for 15 to 60 minutes before cooking.

Cut the tips off the beans and string them if necessary. Steam them just until tender and set aside. Bring at least 6 quarts water to a boil for the pasta.

For sauce, melt butter with olive oil in a heavy large sauté pan. Add the onion and garlic and cook over medium heat just until the onion turns transparent, taking care not to burn the garlic or it will be bitter. Add the green pepper, lemon, basil, and parsley, stir for a minute or two, then add the tomatoes. Simmer just until thickened to a sauce consistency, about 5 minutes. Taste for seasoning and add salt and pepper if desired.

Add 2 tablespoons salt and 1 tablespoon oil to the pasta water. Cook the pasta for just 30 seconds or so, testing it for doneness after 15 seconds. Drain and

place on one half of a warm platter. Arrange beans on the other side of the platter. Spoon the tomato sauce down the center and serve immediately.

To prepare in advance: Uncooked avocado pasta may be covered tightly with plastic wrap and kept in the freezer for up to 8 hours (longer and it may discolor). The sauce may be stored in the refrigerator for up to 4 days and reheated. Steam the beans, cook the pasta, and reheat the sauce just before serving.

Black Cherry Sorbet with Dark Rum 6 small servings

This isn't a sorbet in the traditional sense, made with a sugar syrup and frozen in a *sorbetière*. Instead, frozen black cherries are crushed to a slushy consistency in a food processor without the addition of sugar. Any sweet fruit that has been cut into bite-size pieces and frozen may be substituted; we especially like a combination of strawberries, bananas, and Grand Marnier.

1   *pound sweet pitted black cherries, frozen (see Note)*

¼   *cup fresh orange juice*

2   *tablespoons Myers's dark rum*

    Finely grated orange rind and sprigs of fresh mint (garnish)

Note: If fresh cherries are not available, use the frozen unsweetened ones sold in most supermarkets. Even fresh cherries must be frozen to give this dessert the desired consistency.

Combine cherries, orange juice, and rum in a food processor fitted with the steel blade. Process to a puree, stopping the motor from time to time to push the mixture into the blade with a rubber spatula. (If a processor is not available, puree fresh or thawed cherries in a blender, then transfer to a freezer container and freeze, whisking every 20 minutes or so, until almost firm.)

Spoon into wine or dessert glasses, sprinkle with orange rind, and garnish with mint sprigs. Serve immediately.

To prepare in advance: Sorbet can be stored up to an hour in the freezer without becoming too solid, as the alcohol in the rum prevents it from freezing hard.

Fresh Fruit with California Zabaglione 6 servings

Zabaglione is a warm Italian dessert made of egg yolks, sugar, and wine that must be whipped to a light froth just before serving. Here we use California sparkling wine instead of the traditional Marsala.

3 *fresh peaches, blanched, peeled, and cut into thick slices, or 3 navel oranges, trimmed of all white membrane and cut into sections, or a mixture of fresh seasonal fruits, cut into bite-size pieces*

1 *tablespoon Grand Marnier or other orange-flavored liqueur of your choice*

1 *cup sparkling white wine*

6 *egg yolks*

½ *cup superfine sugar*

Divide fruit evenly among 6 large wine or Champagne glasses. Sprinkle ½ teaspoon Grand Marnier over each serving of fruit.

Combine the wine, yolks, and sugar in a copper zabaglione pan or any *heavy* pan with rounded corners that can be easily reached by a wire whisk. Place over

medium-high heat and whisk *constantly* (you will be very busy here for 4 to 5 minutes) until the mixture is frothy and will hold a soft peak when the beater is lifted. Remove from heat and *immediately* divide equally over the servings of fruit.

To prepare in advance: Fruit may be placed in serving dishes up to 3 hours ahead of time. Zabaglione must be made just before serving.

A Catered Menu for 30

Hors d'oeuvres passed on trays:

Asparagus Tempura with Apricot Mustard

*Potato and Carrot Pancakes
with Melting Brie and Wine-Poached Pears*

Spicy Shrimp with California Salsa

*Pizza with Smoked Duck, Blue Cheese,
and Red Onions*

*Roasted Garlic
with Dill Toast Points*

*Mesquite-Grilled Breast of Chicken Stuffed
with Wild Mushroom Duxelles*

*Chardonnay or Beaujolais Nouveau
(serve chilled)*

Mélange of Grilled Vegetables

*Garlic Fettuccine
with Roasted Red Peppers and Basil*

Crisp Herb Bread with Tomato Butter

*White Chocolate Charlotte with Raspberry
Purée and Bittersweet Chocolate Sauce*

Los Angeles loves to party, and one of the city's most successful catering companies, which can take credit for a myriad of imaginative entertainment-industry and corporate events, is Parties Plus, headed by a creative foursome: husband-and-wife owners Julie and Michael Loshin, their head chef Robert Willson, and designer/coordinator Toby Cox. Parties Plus is a party production company – it produces entire events, from invitations to decor, to fantasy special effects, for many of the most elaborate occasions Hollywood can dream up. We receive constant updates on this company's doings by friends who have attended their party productions and phone us to rhapsodize about the menu.

During the '84 Summer Olympics, Parties Plus produced 60 parties within 12 days. The party hosted by Olympic Organizing Committee President Peter Ueberroth in honor of International Olympic Committee President Juan Antonio Samaranch was a garden affair featuring strolling musicians and a Los Angeles-themed menu. International Olympic officials and ambassadors from the Olympic nations enjoyed an array of dishes that featured Chilled Tomato Bisque with Mint, Hickory-Smoked Chicken Salad, Pistachio-Studded Filet Mignon, Grilled Swordfish with Salsa, Wild Mushroom Ravioli tossed with Roasted Red Peppers and Garlic, and an assortment of American desserts: Plum Cobbler, Blueberry Ice Cream, and Rhubarb Apple Tarts.

More than the usual number of friends phoned us about the following menu, served as a sit-down dinner for several hundred guests at a political fundraiser. Chef Willson was kind enough to share the recipes, which have been adapted to serve 30 guests in a private home. Because of the company policy of preparing almost all the dishes just before serving on the site, one would definitely require serving and kitchen help to duplicate this meal. It can be served either buffet-style or as a sit-down affair, and it features a Southwestern harvest of beautiful, fresh foods.

Robert suggests serving Beaujolais Nouveau, a fruity wine made from the first fermentation of the grapes, with the grilled chicken. It is traditionally available beginning November 15, and must be drunk within a few weeks and served chilled.

Timetable

A week or more ahead:

Prepare and freeze duxelles.

Make and freeze charlotte.

Prepare and refrigerate chocolate sauce.

Prepare and freeze potato-carrot pancakes.

Prepare wine-poached pears; chill.

Make and freeze pizza dough.

Smoke duck.

Prepare and freeze garlic fettuccine.

Prepare tomato butter; freeze.

Make toast points; freeze.

One to 2 days ahead:

Prepare apricot mustard sauce.

Cook and marinate shrimp.

Marinate chicken breasts.

Prepare sauce and peppers for fettuccine.

Prepare raspberry sauce.

Up to 8 hours ahead:

Blanch asparagus and chill.

Assemble pancakes with Brie and pear.

Stuff chicken breasts and skewer.

Bake onions and marinate vegetables for grilling.

Prepare herb bread for baking; thaw tomato butter.

An hour before guests arrive:

Prepare tempura batter.

Roast garlic.

Start mesquite fire.

Grill tomatoes and onions for pizza topping.

Assemble and bake pizza.

After guests arrive:

Fry asparagus.

Grill chicken and vegetables.

Crisp toast points in oven.

Cook fettuccine; toss with sauce.

Thaw charlotte for 15 minutes before slicing.

Asparagus Tempura with Apricot Mustard Makes 50 individual appetizers (30 servings)

L.A.'s Asian influence is responsible for this unusual combination of textures and flavors.

50 medium asparagus stalks

5 to 6 cups vegetable oil for deep-frying

Apricot mustard dipping sauce:

3 apricots, pitted and chopped (1 cup – see Note)

¾ cup honey

¼ cup sugar

2 cups Dijon mustard

Salt to taste

Batter:

¾ cup all-purpose flour

¼ cup cornstarch

1 tablespoon salt

Pinch of freshly ground black pepper

¾ cup ice water

2 teaspoons baking powder

½ teaspoon baking soda

Note: Two cups apricot preserves may be substituted for the fresh apricots, honey, and sugar in this recipe.

Peel the base of each asparagus spear by inserting a small, sharp paring knife under the thicker skin at the base of the asparagus and cutting toward the tip, making the cut shallower as the skin becomes thinner. This will remove the tough outer skin from the base and render the entire stalks edible. Blanch the peeled asparagus in a very large pot of boiling salted water for 2 to 3 minutes, until bright green but still crisp. Plunge immediately into ice water to cool; blot dry.

To make sauce, combine apricots, honey, and sugar in a small non-aluminum saucepan and bring to simmer over medium heat. Cook, stirring often, for 15 to 20 minutes, or until thickened to the con-

sistency of preserves. Remove from heat and stir in mustard and salt to taste. Cool to room temperature.

Prepare batter by combining flour, cornstarch, salt, and pepper in a medium mixing bowl. Stir in ice water, baking powder, and soda and stir until almost smooth. Keep batter on ice or refrigerate until ready to use.

Heat oil in deep-fat fryer or wok to 375°F. Lightly batter asparagus and deep-fry, a few spears at a time, until golden. Serve immediately with apricot mustard sauce.

To prepare in advance: The apricot mustard sauce may be prepared several days ahead of time and stored in the refrigerator. Blanch the asparagus no more than 24 hours in advance or it will lose its crisp quality and bright color. Prepare batter within 2 hours of use, and keep on ice. Fry batter-dipped asparagus just before serving.

Potato and Carrot Pancakes with Melting Brie and Wine-Poached Pears Makes 40 pancakes (30 servings)

Wine poached pears:

2   *bottles (750 ml each) red Burgundy*

2   *cups sugar*

2   *cinnamon sticks*

2   *tablespoons black peppercorns*

1   *tablespoon freshly grated nutmeg*

1   *tablespoon whole allspice berries*

1   tablespoon whole cloves

6   medium-size firm-ripe pears (Bosc or Bartlett)

Potato and carrot pancakes:

10   medium starchy potatoes (5 pounds)

4   medium carrots

2   large onions

3   medium eggs

¼   cup matzo meal

    Salt and freshly ground black pepper to taste

1   pound Brie cheese (see Note)

    Vegetable oil for frying

Note: Other cheeses may be substituted, such as Blue Castello or Monterey Jack.

To poach pears, combine wine, sugar, and spices in large non-aluminum saucepan. Bring to boil over medium heat, stirring to dissolve sugar. Peel and core the pears. Add pears to saucepan, cover partially, and simmer slowly for approximately 20 to 25 minutes, or until pears are easily pierced with the tip of a knife. Remove pears from poaching liquid and cool (reserve poaching liquid to use again). Cut pears lengthwise into thin wedges.

To make pancakes, peel potatoes, carrots, and onions and grate on a medium grater (a food processor is great for this purpose). Wrap grated vegetables in a clean kitchen towel and wring out as much liquid as possible. Transfer grated vegetables to a large bowl and mix in eggs, matzo meal, and seasonings.

Cut Brie into ¼-inch-thick slices, about 1 inch square.

Heat ¾ inch of oil in heavy large skillet until hot but not smoking. Drop rounded tablespoonfuls of potato mixture into the hot oil to form pancakes and brown well over medium-high heat. Turn to

brown other side. Drain well on paper towels. Place a piece of cheese on top each potato pancake; top with a piece of pear.

To prepare in advance: Poach pears up to a week in advance and refrigerate in their syrup. Freeze pancakes in a single layer on a cookie sheet; when frozen solid, transfer to freezer containers, placing plastic wrap or foil between layers. Do not thaw before cooking. For an extra crisp texture, fry again in oil, then assemble as above (alternatively, reheat pancakes in a preheated 375°F oven until very hot and crisp). Top with cheese and pear and serve immediately.

Spicy Shrimp with California Salsa
Makes about 45 appetizers (30 servings)

Shrimp are cooked and skewered to marinate in a spicy Southwestern salsa, then arranged spoke-fashion around a bowl of salsa for dipping. You may wish to make an extra recipe of salsa to serve with crisp-fried tortilla chips.

45   bamboo skewers (6 inches long)

Shrimp:

¾   cup minced shallots

¾   cup olive oil

3   pounds large shrimp (12 to 15 per pound), shelled and deveined

Tabasco sauce to taste

Salt and freshly ground black pepper to taste

Salsa:

2　pounds medium-size ripe tomatoes (about 8 plum tomatoes preferred)

1　cup canned tomato puree (or crushed tomatoes in tomato puree)

⅔　cup finely chopped onion

6　tablespoons extra-virgin olive oil

2　tablespoons coarsely chopped fresh coriander (cilantro)

2　teaspoons minced fresh serrano chiles, seeds and veins removed

1　teaspoon salt, or to taste

　Freshly ground black pepper

　Pinch of sugar

To cook shrimp, combine shallots and olive oil in sauté pan and cook over medium heat for a few minutes, taking care not to brown shallots. Add shrimp and seasonings and sauté until shrimp turn pink and are just done. Remove from heat and cool. Thread shrimp on skewers.

Combine all ingredients for salsa and pour over shrimp. Chill thoroughly; serve chilled.

To prepare in advance: Cook shrimp and marinate for up to 24 hours.

Pizza with Smoked Duck, Blue Cheese, and Red Onions
Makes 2 pizzas (30 or more appetizer servings)

Duck (or chicken) is smoked over a mesquite fire with a sprinkling of hickory, apple, or grapevine chips, in a California-Chinese manner, and used as a topping for a very unusual appetizer pizza.

2   recipes *Basic Pizza Crust*

Smoked duck:

1   *duck (about 4 pounds) or chicken (about 3 pounds)*

1   *tablespoon chile paste with garlic (see Note)*

2   *oranges, quartered*

1   *bunch fresh herbs (a combination of parsley, basil, and marjoram)*

    Salt to taste

2   *cups raw rice*

2   *cups firmly packed dark brown sugar*

2   *onions, quartered (unpeeled)*

1   *bottle (750 ml) white wine*

2   *cups water*

Topping:

½   *cup extra-virgin olive oil*

12 *medium tomatoes, cut into wedges*

3   *red onions, sliced*

6   *medium garlic cloves, peeled, parboiled 5 minutes, and thinly sliced*

6   *ounces Maytag blue cheese (or other blue-veined cheese), crumbled (1½ cups)*

4   *cups shredded part-skim mozzarella cheese*

Note: This paste of hot red chiles, garlic, and salt is available in 6- to 8-ounce bottles in Asian markets and some supermarkets.

To smoke the duck (or chicken), rinse and dry thoroughly. Rub inside and out with chile paste. Place 4 orange quarters inside cavity along with herbs. Season bird with salt.

Prepare a medium fire of mesquite charcoal or wood in a barbecue or smoker with cover. Meanwhile, soak a large handful of hickory, apple, or grapevine chips in cold water to cover. In a large metal bowl that can be placed directly on the charcoal, combine rice, brown sugar, remaining orange sections, onion sections, wine, and water; stir to combine. (This mixture will create a flavorful smoke that permeates poultry deliciously.) Set bowl on charcoal. Place grill directly on the bowl, and set duck on grill over it. Drain soaked wood chips and scatter over coals. Cover duck with foil and the lid of the smoker; smoke for 5 to 6 hours. (Lift lid and foil toward end of cooking time to check quickly if it is necessary to add water to the bowl – but don't do this too often, or you will lose valuable heat. It is not necessary to tend the coals.) Remove duck and cool. Bone the meat; discard skin and bones. Tear meat into bite-size pieces.

Prepare basic pizza dough as directed in recipe. Place rack in bottom third of oven and preheat to 450°F for 30 minutes before baking.

For topping, stir ¼ cup olive oil into tomatoes and onions. Grill lightly (a barbecue basket is good for ease of handling) over mesquite charcoal.

Brush remaining ¼ cup oil over prepared pizza crusts; sprinkle evenly with sliced blanched garlic. Arrange grilled tomatoes and onions evenly over crusts, followed by duck pieces, blue cheese, and mozzarella.

Bake for 15 to 20 minutes, or until crust is browned and crisp. Let rest at room temperature for 5 minutes before serving. Cut pizza into squares to serve as an appetizer.

To prepare in advance: Pizza can be baked an hour or so before serving, then reheated at 425°F for about 10 minutes, or until hot.

Roasted Garlic with Dill Toast Points 30 servings

Garlic cooked in this manner is very sweet, with no trace of bitterness. The cloves slip easily from their papery wrappings and are spread like butter on herb-flavored toast points. Parties Plus chef Robert Willson serves this as part of a first-course plate along with alder-smoked salmon, duck mousse with truffle, baked California chèvre, and American caviar, all accompanied with dill toast points.

30 large heads **fresh** garlic

1½ cups extra-virgin olive oil

Coarsely cracked black pepper

Salt

¼ cup (about) minced fresh herbs: marjoram, basil, thyme

Dill toast points:

30 slices day-old rye bread

1 pound (4 sticks) butter

1 bunch fresh dill, leaves only

Cut tops off unpeeled heads of garlic, exposing the cloves. Combine olive oil, seasonings, and herbs in a large baking pan or jelly-roll pan. Place garlic in oil cut side down, and allow to soak for at least 30 minutes. Turn garlic heads over so cut side is up and bake in preheated 200°F oven for approximately 1½ hours, or until cloves rise out of the skin.

To make toast points, trim crusts and cut bread diagonally into quarters. Combine softened butter with dill; in small mixing bowl, spread on bread, one side only. Arrange on a cookie sheet and toast in preheated 300°F oven for about 45 minutes, or until golden brown and crisp.

Serve garlic hot, surrounded by toast points. Use a small knife to spread softened garlic cloves on the toast like butter.

To prepare in advance: Toast points may be frozen in an airtight container for up to a month, or stored in the refrigerator or at room temperature for 2 to 3 days. For best flavor, reheat before serving. Bake garlic just before serving.

Variation: Roasted garlic may be squeezed from the skin into a glass storage container and the paste mixed with enough extra-virgin olive oil to prevent drying. Refrigerate for use whenever a mild garlic flavor is desired in recipes.

Mesquite – Grilled Breast of Chicken Stuffed with Wild Mushroom Duxelles 30 servings

Mushroom duxelles, a mixture of chopped mushrooms, shallots, and wine that is cooked almost dry, is often used for flavoring in French cooking. Robert Willson uses his version, which features wild mushrooms, as a stuffing for chicken breasts, for ravioli to be sauced with a fresh red pepper sauce, and as a layer in a California torte encased in puff pastry and embellished with a pastry palm tree.

1   *cup fresh lime or lemon juice*

1   *cup honey*

2   *small onions, sliced*

1   *head roasted garlic, squeezed into a paste (see recipe, this menu)*

30   *small whole chicken breasts, (6 to 7 ounces each), boned but not skinned*

Duxelles (makes 4 cups):

2   *pounds white mushrooms*

1   *pound fresh chanterelle mushrooms*

1   *pound fresh shiitake mushrooms*

1   *cup (2 sticks) butter*

6   *tablespoons olive oil*

1   *cup minced shallots*

½   *cup minced fresh parsley*

1   *teaspoon chopped fresh thyme*

1   *cup red Burgundy*

   Salt and freshly ground black pepper to taste

½   *cup Cognac*

30 *12-inch bamboo or metal skewers*

Combine citrus juice, honey, onions, and roasted garlic in shallow pan large enough to hold chicken breasts. Add breasts and marinate for two hours or longer, turning from time to time.

To make duxelles, rinse and dry mushrooms; trim away any woody stems. Mince mushrooms in food processor, a portion at a time, or in a meat grinder.

Melt butter with olive oil in a heavy large skillet (not cast iron) and stir in mushrooms, shallots, parsley, and thyme. Cook over low heat for approximately 40 to 45 minutes, or until most of moisture has evaporated; the mushrooms will become very dark in color and begin to separate into individual pieces. Stir every 10 to 15 minutes to prevent mushrooms from sticking. Add wine and continue to cook another 2 hours or so, until all liquid has evaporated; at this point mushrooms will be almost black. Add Cognac to the pan, ignite with a match, and shake pan until flame is extinguished. Simmer until all liquid has evaporated and mixture is very dry. Cool, then chill.

Drain chicken. Lift chicken skin and spread approximately 2 tablespoons duxelles over the meat beneath the skin. Fold breast in half to enclose duxelles and seal by "sewing" open edges shut with a 12-inch bamboo or metal skewer.

Grill chicken over medium mesquite fire about 12 minutes on each side, or until meat is no longer pink and is easily pierced with the tip of a knife.

Remove skewers and serve chicken whole or sliced diagonally, surrounded by grilled vegetables (recipe follows).

To prepare in advance: Duxelles may be frozen in an airtight container for several months. Chicken breasts may be stuffed the day before cooking if both meat and duxelles are *cold* (to prevent bacterial growth); keep chilled. Remove from refrigerator 2 hours before cooking and grill just before serving.

Variation: Robert recommends grilling chicken in the same manner with other stuffings, such as California chèvre and roasted red peppers, or Monterey Jack cheese and fresh jalapeño chiles.

Mélange of Grilled Vegetables
30 servings

Though vegetables are not served on skewers, except for buffet-style serving, threading them onto skewers before grilling makes them much easier to handle.

15 *red onions*

30 *bamboo or metal skewers*

30 *small yellow summer squash, sliced into ½-inch circles*

30 *small Japanese eggplant, sliced into ½-inch circles*

15 *tomatoes, halved*

1   cup olive oil

Salt and coarsely cracked black pepper to taste

Preheat oven to 350°F. Peel red onions and halve crosswise. Insert a toothpick horizontally through each onion half to prevent it from separating into layers during cooking. Arrange in a large shallow pan in a single layer and bake for 45 minutes. Remove from oven and cool. Thread onions on skewers with remaining vegetables, distributing evenly. Drizzle with olive oil and season with salt and cracked pepper. Allow to marinate at least an hour before grilling.

Five to 10 minutes before serving, place a mesh screen over mesquite coals and grill vegetables for 5 to 10 minutes, or until lightly charred.

Remove skewers and toothpicks and use vegetables to surround grilled chicken.

To prepare in advance: Undercook the vegetables slightly and keep warm for up to an hour in a low oven.

Garlic Fettuccine with Roasted Red Peppers and Basil
30 servings

Pasta dough is flavored with roasted garlic and sauced with more garlic, fresh herbs, and roasted red peppers.

4   *recipes Fresh Pasta (see index), made with the addition of 8 cloves roasted garlic paste (see recipe, this menu) and cut into fettuccine (¹/₂-inch-wide ribbons), or 4 pounds dried fettuccine*

Sauce:

2   *tablespoons minced garlic*

2	*tablespoons minced fresh basil*
1	*tablespoon minced fresh oregano*
1½	*teaspoons minced fresh thyme*
1½	*cups extra-virgin olive oil*
1½	*cups clarified butter (see Note)*
2	*red bell peppers, roasted, peeled (see Index), and cut into thin strips*
2	*tablespoons minced fresh parsley*

Note: Melt 1 pound butter in a small saucepan over low heat, then let it rest for a minute or two off the heat. Skim any milk solids off the top with a ladle, then carefully pour the clear butter into another container, leaving the rest of the solids in the bottom of the pan. The clear butter you have obtained is called "clarified butter" and it has many uses. It will not spoil as does plain butter, and it can stand a much higher temperature without burning, so it is better for frying. It is used here as a butter-flavored oil to coat the strands of pasta evenly.

For sauce, sauté garlic, basil, oregano, and thyme in ¼ cup olive oil over medium heat for 2 to 3 minutes, taking care not to scorch garlic. Add clarified butter, remaining oil, and peppers and cook over low heat for 10 to 15 minutes to marry the flavors.

Cook pasta in boiling salted water just until al dente. Drain well. Toss with sauce until well combined, then toss with minced parsley.

To prepare in advance: Prepare sauce up to 48 hours ahead, cool to room temperature, and refrigerate. Warm briefly before tossing with cooked pasta. Cook pasta just before serving.

Crisp Herb Bread with Tomato Butter
30 servings

This bread is grilled at the same time as the vegetables.

4   *large French bread baguettes, halved lengthwise. Herb butter (1 pound [4 sticks] butter melted with 1 teaspoon each crushed fresh rosemary, minced fresh thyme, and minced fresh marjoram)*

Tomato butter:

1   *pound (4 sticks) unsalted butter, softened*

2   *medium tomatoes (preferably plum), peeled, seeded, and chopped*

2   *tablespoons tomato puree (or paste)*

2   *tablespoons minced fresh basil*

2   *tablespoons minced shallots*

Brush cut sides of French bread with herb butter.

To make tomato butter, combine all ingredients except shallots in food processor. Add shallots and process briefly, just to blend. Use a rubber spatula to transfer mixture to a piece of waxed paper or foil, distributing it evenly in a log about 1 inch in diameter. Wrap into a smooth roll and chill at least 2 hours, or until serving time.

Grill bread, cut side up, until crisp but not burned. Cut into 2-inch slices and serve with tomato butter.

To prepare in advance: Herb butter and tomato butter will freeze well for a month if wrapped airtight. Butter the bread up to 8 hours ahead and grill just before serving.

White Chocolate Charlotte with Raspberry Puree and Bittersweet Chocolate Sauce 16 servings; make two for 30 servings

One of the prettiest and most delicious desserts ever, this luxurious white mousse is served with a bright ruby-colored raspberry sauce and a rich, dark chocolate sauce, then garnished with a bright green sprig of fresh mint.

Chocolate ladyfingers (makes about 24):

Butter and flour for baking sheets

3 *eggs, separated*

½ *cup superfine sugar*

1½ *teaspoons vanilla*

⅔ *cup all-purpose flour*

½ *cup unsweetened cocoa powder*

1 *cup powdered sugar*

White chocolate mousse:

1 *pound 5 ounces white chocolate, coarsely chopped*

¾ *cup light cream (half and half)*

3 *ounces (¾ stick) unsalted butter, softened*

7 *egg whites, at room temperature*

3½ *cups heavy cream*

Raspberry puree:

2 *baskets fresh raspberries*

¼ *cup sugar*

Bittersweet chocolate sauce:

½ *pound bittersweet chocolate (preferably Belgian), coarsely chopped*

1   ounce unsweetened chocolate, coarsely chopped

1   cup heavy cream

¼   cup (½ stick) unsalted butter, cut up

2   tablespoons light corn syrup

30 sprigs fresh mint, to garnish

Note: You will need two 10-inch springform pans to make two of these for 30 guests.

Chocolate ladyfingers are used to line pan in which charlotte is molded. To make them, coat two heavy baking sheets with butter and flour. Adjust racks to divide oven in thirds, and preheat oven to 325°F.

Beat egg whites until they hold firm peaks. Add superfine sugar and continue beating for 1 minute. Without cleaning beaters, beat yolks until light and lemon-colored. Using a large rubber spatula, fold in vanilla, followed by beaten yolks. Gradually sift flour and cocoa over the mixture, folding it in as you go.

Fit a large pastry bag with a plain tube about ⅝ inch in diameter and fill with the mixture. Pipe onto prepared baking sheets in strips about 4 inches long and 1 inch wide, spacing them approximately 1 inch apart. Sprinkle powdered sugar through a sieve to coat ladyfingers thoroughly; let stand 5 minutes. Sprinkle again with sugar and let stand 5 minutes. Bake for 12 to 15 minutes, or until the surface is firm to the touch. Let cool at room temperature for 15 minutes, then remove from the baking sheets; they should slide off easily.

Line a 10-inch springform or charlotte mold with plastic wrap. Arrange ladyfingers around the sides, trimming them as needed to fit pan snugly.

To make mousse, combine white chocolate and light cream in large heatproof mixing bowl over a pan of hot, not boiling, water. Whisk until chocolate has melted and mixture is smooth. Remove from heat and beat in softened butter. Set aside.

Beat whites in very large, grease-free bowl until stiff but not dry. Fold in chocolate mixture. Whip cream until it holds soft peaks (do not overbeat); fold it into chocolate mixture. Pour into prepared pan. Press plastic wrap into surface of mousse and freeze.

To make raspberry puree, put the berries through food mill or puree in blender. Transfer to medium saucepan over medium heat. Stir in sugar and simmer slowly for 5 to 10 minutes, or until thickened to sauce consistency.

Strain puree through dampened cheesecloth to remove seeds. Cool.

To make chocolate sauce, combine chocolates in double boiler top over hot, not boiling, water just until melted. Heat cream and pour over melted chocolate. Whisk in butter and corn syrup. Cool. (For ease in serving, Robert stores sauces in squeezeable plastic bottles.)

Remove charlotte from freezer 15 minutes before serving. Wrap briefly in a kitchen towel that has been rinsed in hot water, then remove sides of springform. Cut into thin wedges and serve on chilled dessert plates. Garnish with the two sauces and a sprig of fresh mint.

To prepare in advance: Freeze charlotte for up to a month. To store ladyfingers separately without drying out, place bottoms of two ladyfingers together and layer between sheets of waxed paper in an airtight container; freeze for up to a month. Raspberry sauce may be refrigerated for up to a week, chocolate sauce for up to a month.

The L.A. Restaurant Style

There is no doubt that a Los Angeles style does exist on the restaurant scene today. Its mark is strictly Southern California, following no specific or traditional patterns. Its guidance comes from everywhere – France's *nouvelle cuisine,* Italy's *alta cucina,* American regionalism, even Southern California's obsession with health. A giant force in shaping L.A.'s culinary style has been influences from our neighbors: Mexico's multifarious cooking and the cornucopia of cuisines brought by the ever-growing Oriental immigrant populations on our shores. The ideas come also from the incredibly abundant food supply at close hand, from the farmlands of Southern, Central, and Northern California. But perhaps most important is the psychological freedom each individual senses to create without limits or restrictions, which is, after all, not only California's legacy to all who live and work in its environment – it's the American way. Never have kitchens anywhere been as democratic, as experimental.

Each chef's interpretation is his or her own, whether the chef is American, Japanese, French, or Thai. And the wonderful thing about it is that L.A. cuisine is continually on the march, evolving, ever-changing, moving ahead to new frontiers, with no end in sight.

For the moment, however, the cuisine can be termed "eclectic."

There is Trumps's Michael Roberts, who, in our opinion, epitomizes the L.A. chef more than any other, doing a salad decidedly French, Mexican, and Oriental. He ties Italian pasta in a Japanese knotting motif and fries it. He combines risotto with shiitake mushrooms and okra. He adds grapefruit to catfish and hushpuppies.

And there is Japanese-born, American-educated Roy Yamaguchi, doing things at 385 North that no one has heard of before. A duck salad comes with Japanese pork *gyoza,* papaya, and a French raspberry-walnut dressing.

There is John Sedlar of Saint Estèphe, who started out as a passionately French nouvelle chef, discovering culinary roots in Santa Fe ideas. Now his cuisine is a marriage of French methods and Santa Fe flavors. What you have is soufflé with chiles verdes, roast squab stuffed with mousse of turkey and pumpkin seeds. Corn tortillas, caviar, and sour cream. The list goes on.

There are Jeffrey Fields of Les Anges and Piero Selvaggio of Valentino, providing food and service so refined as to assure the ultimate dining experience.

Japanese restaurateurs have also left their mark on the L.A. scene by bringing Gallic grace notes to their Oriental themes. French-trained Japanese chefs, such as La Petite Chaya's executive chef Susumu Fukui, perform miracles with French sauces and Japanese culinary artistry. A sheet of translucent agar covers an asparagus vinaigrette to give the effect of grass shoots beneath a blanket of snow.

Even traditional restaurants, such as the bistros — Bistango, Le Chardonnay, and Seventh Street Bistro — change their approach for Los Angeles. Their environment turns joyously upbeat and cheerful, streamlined and carefree, the food light and brighter.

There are some restaurants whose interpretation of L.A. cuisine is purist in nature. So we have Michael's, which brings Maui onions from Hawaii, shiitake and chanterelles grown on California soil, and fish from the Pacific. And we have one restaurateur who thinks of L.A. cuisine as an interpretation of American regional cooking.

Probably no stylist has made a more important impact on the California school than Wolfgang Puck, with his two major Los Angeles restaurants, Spago and Chinois on Main. Both venerate innovation. Both express it with ultimate charm and wit. Spago was the first to lift pizzas out of the Formica-counter parlor to an elitist plane and to serve pastas with such derring-do; Chinois on Main became the first to bring lighthearted charm to an Oriental idea.

California's health food movement, which has traveled across the nation (and now the world), has played some role in the state of the art in Los Angeles's restaurant development. Tommy Tang, whose uncanny perceptions of Western taste have set his restaurant apart from other Thai establishments, is attuned to the health-consciousness of his clientele. He makes sure that his tables are equipped with low-sodium soy sauce and offers up such things as brown as well as white rice.

The veritable food revolution taking place throughout America during this last decade is manifest in the multimillion-dollar food emporia dotting the country from coast to coast. The emporium concept is epitomized full force at Panache. The charm of the European open market is there, with its expensive and exclusive enticements to try everything from pizza to bagels, to Italian style gelati made with tofu.

The aesthetic statement has also become part of today's restaurant scene in Los Angeles, and no restaurant embodies pure artistry better than Katsu, with its Japanese gourmet specialties brought to the table on exquisite ceramic pottery crafted by Japanese artists. The artistic statement is also apparent architecturally; some noteworthy exponents are the Seventh Street Bistro and Rex, which practically outdoes Versailles in its spectacular beauty.

So there you have it. Los Angeles style. The following are not intended to be a comprehensive listing of the great Los Angeles restaurants, nor are they restaurant reviews. They are, to our minds, the restaurants that best represent the current unique Los Angeles style.

Les Anges

14809 Pacific Coast Highway, Santa Monica. 213-454-6521

This restaurant, peeping like a small tugboat from its berth behind the Pacific Coast Highway, has turned out to be quite a surprise.

On the surface, it is French. Stark and streamlined with mirrors and other trompe l'oeil tricks, the place seems larger and more attractive than it really is.

Initially, the food may appear French, but chef Patrick Jamon, former *chef cuisinier* under Claude Peyrot at Vivarois in Paris, will tell you that it is not completely so. "You cannot cook French in Los Angeles," he says. He has educated himself as to the palate of the Los Angeles diner, who seems to take to things grilled and plain, by observing and asking. The name of the restaurant says it all – *Les Anges,* of course, is the French equivalent of "Los Angeles."

His menu tells you how he thinks. There is a hot lamb salad with mustard and herb dressing over a frilly mattress of radicchio, mâche, red leaf lettuce – and maybe three or four other lettuces. He prepares a main course of ravioli filled with lobster served in a pool of superb lobster sauce. He makes a soufflé baked in a sea urchin shell inspired by the ocean outside his window. He serves a brochette of scallops, clams, and shrimp marinated in a lime and herb sauce – quite plain, but the harmony of flavors, texture, and taste is there. Los Angeles-associated ingredients – shiitake mushrooms, California goat cheese, California red and yellow peppers, duck breasts (produced especially for fine French restaurants on farms near Los Angeles) have entered Jamon's cuisine too, and they appear with regularity in specials such as goat cheese and spinach in flaky pastry, and ragout of mussels and shiitake mushrooms. He does duck breast as a duck salad with raspberries, and veal medallions are served with

yellow pepper sauce. Won tons, inspired by the
Oriental cuisine across the ocean, receive the Jamon
interpretation: Won ton wrappers, cut into rounds,
are filled with clam and leek puree and served with
a black bean-ginger sauce.

There seems to be no end to Jamon's penetrating
perception of Los Angeles taste, and if any two
dishes say so, they are this red snapper made with
citrus-wine sauce garnished with California citrus,
and a sole sauce with red wine and bacon.

Poisson aux Trois Citrons
(Fish with Three Citrus Fruits) 2 servings

This is an example, using California citrus as
flavoring and garnish, of the simple fish preparations
found at Les Anges.

1 orange

1 lemon

1 lime

3 tablespoons butter

2 fillets of red snapper, sole or sand dabs

1 medium shallot, minced

½ cup dry white wine

Use a zester to remove outer skin of orange, lemon,
and lime in long, thin strips. Place in a small saucepan and add cold water to cover. Bring to a boil,
then drain and set aside.

Cut each fruit in half crosswise, then cut two thin
crosswise slices from each for garnish. Set aside.
Squeeze juice from remaining fruit for sauce.

Melt 1 tablespoon butter over medium-high heat
in a skillet large enough to hold fish. Add fish and

sauté on both sides just until done (the rule of thumb is 10 minutes per inch thickness). Remove to heated platter and keep warm.

To prepare sauce, pour off excess butter from skillet. Add 1 tablespoon fresh butter. Add shallot and cook until tender but not browned. Add white wine with citrus juice and cook uncovered until reduced to ¼ cup. Whisk in 1 tablespoon cold butter to thicken sauce. Remove from heat. Garnish each plate with reserved slice of orange, lemon, and lime. Pour sauce over fish and top with strips of peel. Serve immediately.

Sole au Vin Rouge (Fish in Red Wine Sauce) 6 servings

A very unorthodox and delicious treatment of fish fillets.

2 pounds sole fillets

Salt and freshly ground white pepper to taste

3 thick slices bacon, cut crosswise into ⅛-inch strips

2 pounds new red potatoes

18 scallions (white part only), cut into 1½-inch lengths

5 tablespoons unsalted butter

2 cups red Burgundy

1 tablespoon fish stock

½ teaspoon fresh lemon juice

3 tablespoons unsalted butter, cut into 3 pieces and chilled

Chopped parsley, to garnish

Rinse fish, pat dry, and season with salt and white pepper.

In a large skillet, cook the bacon until crisp. Drain on paper towels; reserve fat.

Use a sharp paring knife to form the potatoes into 1½-inch ovals. Drop them into boiling salted water for 10 minutes. Drain and pat dry. Sauté the potatoes over low heat in the reserved bacon fat, turning frequently, until they are cooked through and golden brown. When almost done, add the scallions and sauté until lightly browned. Transfer potatoes and scallions to a heatproof platter and keep warm in a low oven with the door ajar.

Pour off the fat from the skillet. Add 5 tablespoons butter and melt over medium heat. When the foam subsides, add the fish fillets, shiny side up. Sauté for 1½ minutes on each side over high heat. Transfer to a heatproof platter and place in oven with the potato-scallion mixture.

Pour off the butter from the skillet. Add the wine and boil over high heat until reduced to about ½ cup, scraping up any bits from the bottom of the pan with a wooden spoon. Add the fish stock and lemon juice.

Turn the heat to low and whisk in the chilled butter pieces, without letting the sauce boil.

Spoon the sauce onto individual serving plates and arrange the fish, potatoes, scallions, and crumbled bacon on top. Sprinkle with parsley and serve.

Bernard's

Biltmore Hotel, 515 South Olive Street, Los Angeles. 213-612-1580

Bernard's is known as one of the "Los Angeles Six," one of the top French restaurants in town. The Los Angeles Six chefs, from Bernard's, Ma Maison, L'Ermitage, L'Orangerie, Le Dôme, and Le St. Germain, are in the L.A. limelight, presenting dinners, teaching other chefs advanced French culinary techniques, and giving courses on how to stuff squab or make chocolate truffles.

Bernard's, in the old Biltmore Hotel, is located in the downtown business section and caters chiefly to businesspeople; however, nothing is ordinary here. Everything surprises, from the ultramodern Bauhaus decor to the food. Under the leadership of Bernard Jacoupy, the director of food and beverages, executive chef Roland Gibert's cooking is "neoclassic," meaning that it is classically French with modern nouvelle overtones. There are country overtones, too, because of Gibert's country background. (He once served a dessert from his childhood in Central France's Aurillac consisting of an apple baked in a pastry case that itself looked like an apple.)

The emphasis at Bernard's is on fish. A lobster salad is served with spinach and grapefruit. Scallops are bathed in an orange cream sauce. Even Gibert's passion for rustic cabbage translates into a fish dish: We are charmed with an entree made of cabbage stuffed with lobster and fish. The crayfish on the platter is probably Gibert's symbolic logo.

We like their treatment of scallops, as follows:

Les Coquilles St.-Jacques à la Vapeur (Steamed Scallops with Vermouth Sauce) 4 to 6 servings

Steam-cooking was first introduced to us at Bernard's, and this fish dish typifies the technique.

3 *bunches parsley*
4 *ounces (1 stick) unsalted butter*

2   *tablespoons chopped shallot*

1   *cup dry vermouth*

1   *cup heavy cream*

   Salt and freshly ground pepper

2   *pounds scallops*

Separate parsley leaves from stems, reserving stems to flavor scallops during steaming. Blanch leaves in boiling water to cover for 30 seconds. Drain, pressing out excess liquid. Place parsley leaves in food processor and chop finely. Set aside.

Melt 1 teaspoon butter in a large skillet. Add shallot and sauté until just tender. Add vermouth and cook until almost absorbed. Add cream and return to a boil. Add remaining butter bit by bit, whisking lightly until sauce is smooth and butter is melted; do not boil. Remove from heat and season to taste with salt and pepper.

Add water to steamer pot to a level below the steamer rack. Add parsley stems and salt to taste. Bring to a boil. Reduce heat. Place scallops in steamer rack, cover, and steam over simmering water, being sure water does not touch rack, for about 3 minutes or until scallops are just opaque. Place bed of chopped parsley on serving plate. Arrange scallops over parsley and top with vermouth sauce. Serve immediately.

Bistango

133 North La Cienega Boulevard, Los Angeles.
213-652-7788

Bistango has a name like an exotic bird, but it really means bistro. And what a bistro it is – packed by day and night, which means, of course, that it is speaking to its Los Angeles audience. Atmosphere, food, and feeling are strictly L.A. The restaurant has the colors of a beautiful Southern California day: mauve, peach, and grey. The feeling is open and fresh, with a decor of glass, tile, wood, and oversized plants.

The place has a dual personality: part café, part restaurant. The café portion is dominated by a bar open until 1 a.m., and the food served is pastas, pizzas and calzones, neither French nor Italian. They are as Californian as the decor, using the nouvelle thumb-size vegetables that have settled nicely into restaurant cooking today. The bistro cooking by chef Claude Segal (formerly with Ma Maison) appears hard-core French, but the touch is light. No pig's knuckles, caul, or heavy sauces here. The café serves specials like *cassoulet* and *choucroute,* and such other bistro standbys as grilled duck, grilled chicken with mustard sauce, and salads, including a California Chinese chicken salad for light eaters.

The more leisurely restaurant area serves up things like mussels steamed in white wine, timbales of eggplant, preserved duck and cabbage salad, veal tenderloin, and crisp *goujonnettes* of John Dory, a New Zealand fish, in crayfish sauce.

If there is such a thing as a California obsession with dessert, and there is — contradicting notions of health and fitness — no one has a better grasp of it than Bistango, where New Wave young and over-40s alike dip into Blue Moons, one of the many sundaes made with passionfruit sherbet in blue Curaçao; Napoleon circles; and Marquis au Chocolat.

Still, it's the simplicity of the cooking that Los Angeles diners like. And one of the nicest dishes is this bistro specialty, duck breast served over wild mushrooms.

Salmis de Canard au Zinfandel et aux Champignons Sauvages (Duck Breasts in Zinfandel Sauce with Wild Mushrooms) 6 servings

Zinfandel and veal stock, slow-simmered to a syrupy glaze becomes an elegant and rich-tasting sauce.

12 ounces fresh wild mushrooms (such as cèpes or shiitake)

2 large ducklings, cut up

2 shallots, chopped

1 bottle (750 ml) Zinfandel

4 cups veal stock (see Index)

Several parsley sprigs

Salt and freshly ground black pepper

½ cup (1 stick) chilled unsalted butter

Remove stems from mushrooms. Mince stems; set caps aside. Brown duck necks over high heat for 10 minutes. Add minced mushroom stems and sauté until pan liquids are brown. Add shallots and sauté 1 minute. Pour Zinfandel into pan and bring to a boil. Boil vigorously until liquid is reduced to a glaze. Add veal stock, parsley, and salt and pepper to taste. Bring to a simmer and simmer over medium heat 30 minutes, or until reduced to a syrupy glaze.

Set aside all but the duck breasts for another use. Sauté duck breasts over high heat for 15 to 20 minutes, turning often, until browned; they should be rare inside (cook longer to desired doneness, if you wish). Remove from heat and set aside.

Strain Zinfandel sauce through fine strainer. Whisk in ½ stick butter, cut into small pieces, and remove from heat. Keep sauce warm in double boiler over hot (not simmering) water; do not overheat or sauce will separate.

Melt remaining butter in another pan. Add mushroom caps and sauté over high heat just until tender.

Cut cooked duck breasts into thin slices. Spread mushroom caps on platter. Arrange sliced duck breasts on top of mushrooms and nap with Zinfandel sauce.

Le Chardonnay

8284 Melrose Avenue, Los Angeles. 213-655-8880

Sweet, charming, and pristine in its Art Nouveau style, the mood created by scrolly rosewood moldings, shimmering tiles, marble floors, and high mirrored walls reflects exactly the restaurant's intent of bringing the customer back to times when life was unhurried and more gentle. Strangely enough, though, Le Chardonnay makes an *au courant* statement, expressing the sophisticated taste of Los Angeles diners who occasionally like dipping into this small-scale clone of the Vagenende in Paris and eating its very fresh, thoroughly honest French bistro food when the mood strikes. And why not? The cooking is done by Claude Alrivy, who was executive chef for over 12 years at Le St. Germain, another fine Los Angeles eatery. We'd go any time for the wonderfully substantial onion tart or for the fat and flavorful herb omelets with snails sautéed in garlic. Le Chardonnay is big on grilled things, done on a handsome brass and tiled rotisserie. Among the more interesting grilled dishes on which Le Chardonnay prides itself are the John Dory with onion marmalade and tomato, the New York steak with Brouilly wine sauce, and baby chicken stuffed with blanched garlic. Nor should one miss desserts at Chardonnay, especially not the apple fritters with

apricot sauce, and the coffee is very good. The wine list is loaded, of course, with French and California Chardonnays.

The following recipe exemplifies Le Chardonnay's bistro-style cooking.

Warm Sweetbread Salad with Snow Peas and Oyster Mushrooms
4 servings

1   *veal sweetbread (2 lobes)*

2   *tablespoons fresh lemon juice* or *white vinegar*

1   *tablespoon salt*

32   *snow peas*

Vinaigrette dressing (made of 1 tablespoon peanut oil, 1 teaspoon wine vinegar, and salt and freshly ground black pepper to taste)

1½   *pounds fresh oyster mushrooms*

6   *tablespoons peanut oil*

2   *tablespoons (¼ stick) butter*

Wash sweetbread gently in cold water. Place in large bowl and cover with cold water to which you have added 1 tablespoon lemon juice or white vinegar; soak for 1½ hours. Drain and gently peel off as much of the thin outer membrane as possible. Remove and discard the tube from the sweetbread, separating the two lobes. Cover with fresh cold water, to which you have added 1 tablespoon lemon juice or white vinegar, and soak 1½ hours longer. Peel off any remaining membrane. Blanch sweetbread by placing in a saucepan with water to cover and 1 tablespoon salt and bringing to a boil. Drain immediately and rinse under cold water to stop cooking process.

Remove strings from peas and blanch in boiling salted water for a minute or two, until bright green and crisp-tender; plunge into cold water to stop the cooking. Blot dry and toss with vinaigrette.

Peel the oyster mushrooms. Heat 3 tablespoons peanut oil in large skillet over high heat and sauté mushrooms for 2 minutes; drain well.

Just before serving, melt butter in medium skillet (preferably nonstick) and sauté mushrooms over medium-high heat for 3 minutes, seasoning with salt and pepper. Heat remaining 3 tablespoons peanut oil in another medium skillet. Cut each sweetbread lobe into 4 slices and sauté in oil over medium-high heat for 1 minute on each side, or until lightly browned.

Divide mushrooms among four serving plates, mounding them in the center. Surround mushrooms with snow peas, eight to a plate. Place 2 sweetbread slices on top of each serving of mushrooms and serve immediately.

La Petite Chaya

1930 Hillhurst Avenue, Los Angeles. 213-655-5991

Chaya Brasserie

8741 Alden Drive, Los Angeles. 213-859-8833

The Franco-Japanese influences that have set Los Angeles-style cooking apart from the rest of the nation are both inescapable and exemplary at the Chayas. Executive chef Susumu Fukui, trained in both classical Japanese cuisine *(kappo)* and *haute cuisine française* at the Imperial Hotel in Tokyo, brings the culinary challenges of East and West to a highly artistic plane at both the restaurant and the new brasserie several miles away.

The restaurant, in an out-of-way spot in Los Feliz, is unexpectedly inviting with its bare pastel look. The cooking is highly original. The salads boggle the mind: Crisp wonton skins are layered with asparagus, raw tuna, and mustard vinaigrette. A roll of salmon mousse is covered with paper-thin daikon. Paupiettes of seafood are wrapped in Japanese rice paper.

At the brasserie, the bistro food is a provocative California-Oriental-Milanese. Fukui's chef, Hidemasa Yamamoto, whose Italian restaurant training inspired the pastas served at the brasserie, serves ravioli with stuffed shrimp and tagliarini with smoked salmon. One finds smoked eel salad, sliced giant clams on a bed of chicken and cabbage salad, and roast duck breasts done up with both French and Japanese sauces. Atmosphere at the brasserie, designed around a large central atrium, is fitting, too. The feeling is contemporary and the details Oriental: basic black and white, large mirrors, chinoiserie paintings on plywood, silk lighting fixtures, and bamboo reaching toward the skylight.

Cigares de Poulet au Curry à la Chaya (Baked Spring Rolls Stuffed with Chicken and Mushrooms)
approximately 100 appetizers

2   *small chickens (about 1¼ pounds each) or 3 whole chicken breasts*

8   *ounces (2 sticks) butter*

1   *medium onion, minced*

12 *mushrooms, cleaned and minced*

2	garlic cloves, minced
½	cup dry white wine
2	tomatoes, peeled, seeded, and chopped
2	teaspoons curry powder
2	cups heavy cream
	salt and freshly ground white pepper to taste
100	won ton skins (about 1 pound)

Cut chicken into 1-inch pieces and mince finely, either by feeding it through a meat grinder or chopping, 1 cup at a time, by pulsing the motor on and off.

In a large heavy skillet, melt the butter and saute the onion, mushrooms, and garlic until the onion is transparent and the liquid from the mushrooms has evaporated. Add the ground chicken, tomatoes, and white wine. Boil over medium-high heat until the liquid is almost completely evaporated. Add the curry powder and salt and pepper; cook 1 minute. Add cream and cook until mixture is smooth and thick. Remove from heat and cool.

Wrap the mixture in won ton skins in the manner of spring rolls (dampen corners of skin with cold water, place about 1½ teaspoons of filling on one corner and rolling into a smooth cigar-shaped roll, tucking in the outside corners as you roll).

Arrange on baking sheet and bake, seam-side down, at 375°F, for 10 to 15 minutes, or until golden brown.

To prepare in advance: Freeze on baking sheets, and when firm transfer to bags for freezer storage. It is not necessary to thaw before baking.

Chinois on Main

2709 Main Street, Santa Monica. 213-392-9025

"I never considered myself a trend-setter. I just get bored very easily."

— Wolfgang Puck

Wolfgang Puck is hailed by restaurant critics around the world as "one of the most innovative chefs in the USA." He was once head chef and part owner of Ma Maison, has created and owns Spago in Los Angeles and Japan, and now, here's another prize Puck restaurant – a whim, actually with decor that startles the eye with its craziness. A snake-like enamel jade bar undulates across the room. Out-sized art nouveau moldings, a gilded Buddha, cloisonne cranes, profusions of flowers come at you from all directions. The restaurant concept Puck's – "Hey, let's do something Chinese," just like that. The decor was his wife Barbara's.

This really isn't Chinese cuisine at all. It's pure Los Angeles, a made-up cuisine which expresses with frivolity the growing trend toward *nouvelle chinoise.* If there is any doubt about the fervor of the *nouvelle-chinoise* mania in Los Angeles, try coming here at midnight. You may get in. Then again, you may not.

Kazuto Matsusuka, who now heads the kitchen, comes up with extraordinary things. Wok-fried redfish with everchanging sauces is one of his specialties. Oysters, glistening in their shells, are served on a bed of salt with pools of curry sauce. Mongolian lamb is laced with a sauced mixture of cilantro, parsley and mint, more Middle than Far Eastern.

We love to sit at the counter in the back of the room and watch with fascination as the chefs in the exposed kitchen dash from gas range to a line of woks and back again in a wild dance of culinary

creativity. The following recipe is one of our favorites.

Sizzling Catfish 4 servings

This is the most popular dish at Chinois – floured catfish, deep-fried and brought to the table looking gorgeous on a huge black platter.

1	*catfish (2 pounds)*
12	*thin slices fresh ginger*
	Salt and freshly ground black pepper
	Cornstarch
	Peanut oil for deep frying

Saké Sauce: (makes ½ cup)

6	*tablespoons unseasoned rice vinegar*
2	*tablespoons saké (see Note)*
1	*tablespoon Japanese soy sauce (see Note)*
	Juice of ½ lemon

Note: Japanese soy sauce is a light soy sauce; Kikkoman is a widely available brand. Saké is Japanese rice wine. Both are available in supermarkets and Japanese markets.

Make six diagonal slits through each side of catfish. Insert a slice of ginger root into each slit. Season fish with salt and pepper to taste. Dust lightly with cornstarch. Heat oil in large wok to 425°F. Fry fish in hot oil until it is browned on both sides and flesh yields easily when pierced with fork, about 5 minutes. Remove fish from wok and drain on paper towels. Transfer fish to large serving platter.

For sauce, combine ingredients in small bowl and mix well. Serve on the side with fish.

City Café

7407½ Melrose Avenue, Los Angeles. 213-658-7495

City Café was one of the first in Los Angeles
to come up with the no-kitchen restaurant idea.
Owners Gay Gherardi, Margo Willits, and Barbara
McReynolds would purchase the salad from here,
the dessert from there, and put it together as if
it had come from their kitchen. They did up the
tiny, railroad-style place in a pinky-blue Zolatone
look (a spray paint process widely used in the 50's),
threw some consignment art on the walls, and sur-
prised themselves with their cleverness. There is a
kitchen now, run by Mary Sue Milliken and her
friend Susan Feniger, both of whom have some
culinary background.

What you get is interpretative cooking that seems
to be the order of the day among young chefs in
Los Angeles and elsewhere. It is a sort of culinary
sorcery of the unexpected, gleaned from cuisines
around the world or from wherever the cooks
happen to have found inspiration. Melon and
cilantro tossed with a spicy Thai marinade. Portu-
guese mussel stew. Curried lamb stew with yogurt
and rice. Pickled calf's tongue with crayfish sauce
and pears. Vegetable fritters with chickpea batter.
The dishes are interesting, and the high- and low-
life clientele, who are themselves an entertainment,
will be flocking to City Café to see and be seen for
a long time to come.

Anything goes, as you will see in the following recipe.

Grilled Chicken with Bulgur 6 to 8 servings

Grilling has become commonplace in restaurants throughout the city, and City Café does it uncommonly well.

3   chickens (3 pounds each), cut up

Salt and freshly ground black pepper

All-purpose flour

3   green bell peppers

3   yellow bell peppers

6   tablespoons plus 1 teaspoon butter

2   onions, halved lengthwise and thinly sliced

6   shallots, sliced

12   mushrooms, sliced

Pinch of paprika

½   cup dry white wine

1   tomato, coarsely chopped

2   cups (or more) chicken stock

Few drops hot pepper sauce

Cracked Wheat:

2½   cups chicken stock

¼   cup (½ stick) unsalted butter

Salt and freshly ground black pepper

2½   cups cracked wheat (bulgur)

Preheat oven to 375°F. Remove leg and thigh bones from chickens (or have your butcher do this). Trim off tendons and gristle.

Sprinkle chicken lightly with salt and pepper. Dredge lightly in flour, brushing off excess. Place chicken pieces skin side down on heated grill to mark skin in a crisscross pattern, if desired (or heat metal skewers and sear chicken skin in crisscross pattern). Bake for 20 to 30 minutes, or until tender. Set aside and keep warm.

Place green and yellow peppers under broiler until skin is charred and blistered, turning to char evenly. Remove from boiler. Transfer peppers to a closed plastic bag to steam for at least 10 minutes. Remove from bag and peel off skin, rinsing as necessary. Remove cores and seeds from peppers. Cut peppers into julienne strips, reserving any scraps.

Melt 1 teaspoon butter in small skillet. Add onions and cook over low heat, stirring, until golden brown. Add pepper julienne, season to taste with salt and pepper, and set aside.

Melt 2 tablespoons butter in a large heavy skillet over medium heat. Add sliced shallots, mushrooms, reserved green and yellow pepper scraps, and paprika and sauté until vegetables are just tender, taking care not to scorch shallots. Add wine and tomato and simmer uncovered until reduced by half. Add chicken stock and simmer 20 minutes longer.

Meanwhile, cook cracked wheat: Combine stock, butter, and salt and pepper to taste in a heavy saucepan of at least 4-quart capacity. Bring to a boil. Add cracked wheat, bring to a simmer, and cook 3 to 5 minutes. Remove from heat. Completely wrap terrycloth towel around lid, twisting ends into a knot on top of lid to prevent towel from falling, and cover saucepan with the cloth-wrapped lid (cloth will absorb moisture and make wheat fluffy rather than soggy). Let stand to steam in a warm place for 10 to 15 minutes.

When the sauce has finished cooking, puree it in blender or food processor; strain. If sauce is too thick, add more chicken stock (about ½ cup). Season to taste with salt, pepper, and hot pepper

sauce. Whisk in remaining 4 tablespoons cold butter, cut into bits, just until melted; remove from heat.

Spoon cracked wheat into bottom of platter. Top with chicken pieces and ladle sauce over chicken. Garnish with peppers and onions.

La Cucina

7383 Melrose Avenue, Los Angeles. 213-653-8333

What an impact Celestino Drago, the chef at La Cucina, made when he first appeared on the scene at an obscure, offbeat interim café back in 1982. He might be the best Italian chef in Los Angeles; he has the skill, imagination, creativity, authority, and, above all, a grace rare in a chef so young.

Drago's cooking is modern Italian with a strong innovative bent. Would you find his kind of cooking in Rome, Florence, or Naples? Not quite, because Drago is speaking only to Los Angeles with his ideas and ingredients.

He'll try anything and everything: carob pasta, lemon pasta, pasta with olive sauce and smoked mozzarella. He'll make pasta *timballo* (pastry-encased pasta) straight out of the Italian Renaissance, or pasta served from a foil bubble that sends wafts of perfumy Cognac into the air when opened. The pastas are truly remarkable, so we never miss them, even when we plan on having the grilled meats, poultry, and fish. The menu is small, but rotates daily, and among many other choices we love the grilled baby chicken cuddled in a nest of fine-cut French fries, the salmon with sorrel sauce, and the black risotto cooked in squid ink. La Cucina is tiled, marbled, white, and bright; its open kitchen services both the café and old, elegant Chianti next door. La Cucina, however, is more inviting, more

Los Angeles, more today. And if you are ever there, you will find this simplest Italian dish – pasta with tomato and basil sauce – speaking the language of Los Angeles.

Angel Hair Pasta with Fresh Tomato and Basil Sauce 4 servings

This barely cooked sauce is wonderfully fresh-tasting.

6 *large ripe tomatoes, peeled, seeded, and diced*

½ *cup extra-virgin olive oil*

3 *garlic cloves, minced*

1½ *teaspoons chopped fresh oregano or ½ teaspoon dried oregano, crushed*

Salt and freshly ground black pepper

2 *bunches fresh basil, leaves only (2 cups, loosely packed)*

1 *pound angel hair or other pasta*

In a bowl, combine tomatoes, olive oil, garlic, oregano, and salt and pepper to taste. Reserve a few basil leaves for garnish. Chop remaining leaves and add to tomato mixture; set aside.

Cook pasta until al dente; drain. Turn pasta into a large skillet and add tomato mixture. Toss pasta and sauce over high heat for 2 minutes, or until well mixed. Garnish with reserved fresh basil leaves and serve immediately.

Cutters

2425 Colorado Avenue, Santa Monica. 213-453-3588

If there is a place that has something for everybody, Cutters has got to be it. It is by its own definition an American bar, brasserie, restaurant, bistro, and café all in one, offering everything and anything from sashimi, pasta, quiche, focaccia, pizzas, calzones, and Chinese stir-fry dishes to Italian gelato and New Orleans bread pudding. The beverages offered are so varied that you might classify the list as World's-Fair scale: There are regular and decaffeinated espresso, fresh-brewed coffees and teas, herb teas, natural juices, European citrus drinks, waters of every denomination, non-alcoholic beer and wine, demi- and full-shot cocktails, wine by the glass, and a good selection of French, Italian, and American red, white and sparkling wines.

This is the restaurant concept of the future, already in evidence in several large American cities. But there is not the hustle-bustle of the Rockefeller Plaza eatery complex, or that of San Francisco's waterfront or New Orlean's marketplace. The menu, by design, is focused on Los Angeles's eclectic tastes and penchant for good health; in fact, it designates dishes that are particularly low in sodium, fats, and sugars. Ethnic dishes, slightly modified to suit the native palate, include Chinese chicken salad and pastas with unusual, rather off-beat treatments, such as pasta shells stuffed with Cajun-style chicken

The Oriental theme is carried through in dishes such as this novel Yaki Soba, made with Japanese buckwheat noodles, a vegetable mixture of shiitake, carrots, and zucchini, and a soy-ginger sauce.

Yaki Soba with Chicken 1 serving

At Cutters this is also served with shrimp, pork or no meat at all.

¼ cup Japanese soy sauce

¼ cup saké

¼ cup unseasoned rice vinegar

1 teaspoon sugar

1 small garlic clove, minced

½ teaspoon minced fresh ginger

3 ounces boned and skinned chicken breasts, cut into 1-to 1½-inch pieces

9 ounces soba noodles (see Note)

3 tablespoons sesame oil

1 small carrot, cut into julienne strips

½ small onion, cut into ¼-inch-thick slices

Salt and freshly ground black pepper

½ small zucchini, cut into 1½ x ⅛ x ⅛-inch pieces

1 shiitake mushroom, cut into ¼-inch slices

2 tablespoons peeled jicama, cut into 1½ x ½ x ½-inch pieces

Pinch of Japanese chile pepper blend (nanami togarashi)

1 teaspoon minced scallion

1 teaspoon grated red pickled ginger

Note: Japanese ingredients may be purchased in Japanese markets and many supermarkets in Southern California. Soba are buckwheat noodles, nanami togarashi is a chile pepper blend, Japanese soy sauce is a light soy sauce (Kikkoman is a widely available brand), and saké is rice wine.

Combine soy sauce, saké, vinegar, sugar, garlic, and ginger in small bowl. Add chicken and turn to coat well. Marinate several hours or overnight. Drain, reserving marinade.

Drop noodles into enough boiling water to cover and boil for 2 minutes. Rinse in cold water. Drain well and set aside.

Preheat griddle or large skillet. Add 2 tablespoons sesame oil. Place carrot, onion, and noodles on griddle. Toss until vegetables are just crisp-tender and noodles are heated through, 1 to 2 minutes. Season to taste with salt and pepper. Push to one side of griddle. Add chicken to hot griddle and season to taste with salt and pepper. Cook 3 minutes, or until golden brown on one side. Turn and cook 1 to 2 minutes, or until golden brown on other side; do not overcook. Place zucchini, mushroom, and jícama over noodles. Drizzle 1 tablespoon sesame oil over all ingredients, along with any remaining marinade. Cook until sauce evaporates and begins to caramelize, moving noodles back and forth over griddle surface until well browned. Mound mixture on warm serving plate. Garnish top with a sprinkling of *togarashi,* scallion, and pickled ginger.

Katsu

1972 Hillhurst Avenue, Los Angeles. 213-665-1891

There is no name on the door. The only distinguishing landmark is a couple of granite rocks placed at either side of the door. Katsu, a restaurant and sushi bar, makes a dramatic statement, stark and simple, with no flourishes except for the fabulous artwork on the walls and extraordinary floral arrangements.

No California roll here. The classical Japanese food is uncompromisingly authentic, completely fresh, indescribably beautiful to look at, pleasantly shocking and, for most Americans, a new experience. In fact, what draws Los Angeles diners to Katsu is the rare combination of high-performance cuisine within a high-tech modern context.

There is no menu and the specials, recited by young Japanese waiters wearing New Wave costumes and long, thin ties, are changed weekly. But one can expect seafood, served up as never before: sautéed abalone served with an egg-vinegar sauce, whole crab stuffed with egg and deep-fried, shell and all. A seafood plate of barbecued oysters, scallops, and shrimp comes on a shiny black plate with a garnish of ginger stick and orange wedge. A lobster tail prepared tempura-style rests upright on its red shell. A whole trout appears to be twisting in motion on the plate. Every plate is a picture. For tamer tastes, there is always steak teriyaki, tempura, and *shabu shabu,* which will come with crab, not beef. There is sushi prepared by owner Katsu Michite and protégés, served both at the sushi bar and at the tables. The table sushi comes magnificently arranged on long ceramic trays crafted by Japanese artist Mineo Mizumo. The temptation is to order everything, including this extraordinary creation of red snapper stuffed with tofu and mixed vegetables, which lies on a platter over a silver origami.

Red Snapper Stuffed with Tofu 4 servings

Slices of stuffed snapper are served with sliced fresh ginger root and a variety of mint called *shiso,* but fresh mint can be substituted.

½   *cup vegetable oil*

2   *tablespoons diced burdock root (canned or fresh)*

1   *small carrot, diced*

1   *shiitake mushroom, chopped*

½   *cup chopped bamboo shoot*

1   *package (14 ounces) tofu*

1   *teaspoon sesame oil*

½   *cup sugar*

½   *cup mild soy sauce*

1   *teaspoon salt*

1   *red snapper fillet (1 pound)*

Mild Sauce (see below)

Shiso *leaves or fresh mint leaves (optional garnish)*

Sliced ginger root (optional garnish)

Heat oil in large skillet. Add burdock root, carrot, mushroom, and bamboo shoot and sauté until just tender. Add tofu and sesame oil and mix well. Combine sugar, soy sauce, and salt and add to tofu mixture; mix well. Place fillet on clean surface, skin side down. Spread with tofu mixture and roll up jelly-roll fashion. Fasten seam with wood or bamboo picks. Place on steamer rack over simmering water, being careful water does not touch rack. Steam 5 to 6 minutes, or until fish is just opaque. Slice stuffed snapper into 4 equal portions. Serve with Mild Sauce. Garnish with *shiso* leaves or mint leaves and ginger root, if desired.

Mild Sauce (makes about 1 quart):

32   *ounces* dashi *(Japanese dried fish stock made from a mix)*

½   *cup mild soy sauce*

Salt

2   *teaspoons* kuzu *(see Note), or 4 teaspoons arrowroot*

Note: Kuzu is a powdered starch made from the kuzu wine, and is sold in Japanese markets and

health-food stores. Use as you would arrowroot powder, but use only half as much.

Combine *dashi,* soy sauce, and salt to taste in saucepan and bring to a boil. Mix kuzu or arrowroot with a small amount of water until smooth. Stir some of the hot liquid into cornstarch mixture, then return to hot liquid. Cook and stir until a thin sauce is formed.

Michael's

1147 Third Street, Santa Monica. 213-451-0843

Where do you start with Michael's, the king of the California-French restaurant? Michael's is a must on every out-of-town food-lover's list of places in Los Angeles to try. Ubiquitous Michael McCarty (you'll know him by his slicked-back Noël Coward hair and fast talk) has been a major force in promoting California cuisine to the rest of the nation, if not the world. And, like Wolfgang Puck, he puts his money where his mouth is, by encouraging local farmers to develop new products that set us apart from the rest of the nation and by pushing other restaurants to make use of them. It was he who promoted restaurant use of baby vegetables and some hybrids grown by specialty farmers. His culinary style has been copied widely by others, but the Michael's French-California stamp is inimitable. It's formal, yet casual, loosened up like a tie broken from its knot. There are grilled meats, fish, and poultry with crispy French fries or fried Maui onion rings. Dishes are served in "nouvelle" portions (smaller and more expensive than most is a frequent complaint). Then there are the California-grown products, such as shiitake and chanterelles, Montrachet-style goat cheese, and even goat meat, oysters, specially-grown ducks, and great varieties of Pacific coast fish and shellfish done up imaginatively by whomever the chef might be. (Celebrity chef Jonathan Waxman,

now of Jams in New York, got his first big break at Michael's.) McCarty's restaurant reflects the rosy glow of the sand and the openness of the ocean nearby. The garden, filled with exotic and rare plants, gets as much attention from McCarty as his kitchen does. One sunny day we lunched on a salad of grilled scallops on a bed of radicchio and butter lettuce topped with raw slices of tuna, tiny *haricots verts* dressed with a ginger, rice vinegar, soy vinaigrette. This was followed by a spectacular dish of angel hair pasta with Chardonnay cream sauce, a few thin slices of Norwegian salmon, red and yellow peppers, golden caviar, sprinkled like confetti with chopped fresh herbs.

You see? Michael loves fresh ingredients, and the following recipe is a superb example of his style.

Chicken and Goat Cheese Salad
6 servings

An unusual dish of chicken stuffed under the skin with goat cheese is delicious and represents the very finest of Southwest ingredients.

12	*ounces California goat cheese, preferably white Montrachet-style, sliced or crumbled*
6	*chicken breast halves, boned (do not skin)*
	Salt and freshly ground black pepper
1/4	*cup Sherry vinegar*
1/2	*cup olive oil*
	Salt and freshly ground pepper
6	*tomatoes, peeled, seeded, and chopped*
1	*bunch fresh coriander* (cilantro), *leaves only, chopped*
1	*jalapeño chile, charred, peeled, and minced*
	Juice of 2 limes

3 heads limestone lettuce

3 bunches mâche

2 bunches arugula

2 heads radicchio

2 heads baby red-leaf lettuce

3 avocados, pitted, peeled, sliced, and fanned

3 red bell peppers, charred, peeled, seeded, and cut
   into wedges

3 yellow bell peppers, charred, peeled, seeded, and cut
   into wedges

2 bunches chives, minced

Stuff goat cheese under skin of chicken breasts. Sprinkle with salt and pepper. Place on barbecue grill or broiler rack about 4 inches from heat source and grill or broil until browned, turning once, about 15 minutes. Slice thinly and keep warm.

Combine vinegar, oil, and salt and pepper to taste in medium bowl. Add tomatoes, cilantro, jalapeño, and lime juice and mix well.

Arrange limestone lettuce, mâche, arugula, radicchio, and red-leaf lettuce on each plate. Place sliced chicken in center of greens. Pour tomato dressing over greens and chicken. Garnish plates with avocado, red and yellow peppers, and chives.

Muse

7360 Beverly Boulevard, Los Angeles. 213-934-4400

The Muse came to Los Angeles whispering, "Give them neo-California." And neo-California it is: just the stone-carved letters M-U-S-E in the threshold of the tomb-like stucco structure.

The design statement is cold, clean, clinical, and handsome with its Navajo white, dusty pink, and muted grey tones – one of a handful of unmistakably Los Angeles-style restaurants considered upbeat and trendy.

What makes Muse uniquely trendy, however, is the food. No need to ask who the chef is. It doesn't really matter. The tone set by the establishment is what is felt, even without a distinctive presence in the kitchen or at the door. Any one of the handsome maitre d's with faces like Calvin Klein models could be one of the owners. But who would know? Muse is a business, not a personality cult. So you will find the menus as impersonal and offbeat as its ambiance suggests. California offbeat, with dishes like onion soup laced with Cognac and topped with Roquefort, New Zealand mussels steamed in white Burgundy and Parmesan cheese, charbroiled pigeon over grilled Japanese eggplant with golden caviar, sashimi of Hawaiian smoked tuna with marinated European cucumbers, grilled tuna with daikon sprouts, and buckwheat *somen* noodles. Every dish is something familiar sparked by the unfamiliar: linguini with cockles; garlic chicken salad with fried Chinese noodles; fresh New Zealand venison roasted with shallots, wild tarragon, and Zinfandel.

Chocolate Gâteau Mousseline 8 servings

Here is Muse's very tender cake, flavored with espresso and unusual in that it contains no flour.

Butter and cocoa powder to coat pan

6 *ounces semisweet chocolate, broken*

1 *ounce unsweetened chocolate, broken*

1 *tablespoon instant espresso mixed with 1 tablespoon water*

½ *cup Cointreau or Grand Marnier*

3	eggs
1/4	cup sugar
1/2	cup heavy cream, whipped to soft peaks
	Powdered sugar, to garnish
1	cup heavy cream, whipped to soft peaks (garnish)

Position rack in center of oven and preheat to 350°F. Butter a 9-inch square baking pan, line bottom with waxed paper, and butter the paper. Dust cocoa evenly over bottom of pan.

Melt chocolates with espresso in double boiler top or heatproof bowl placed over hot, not boiling, water. Remove from heat, add Cointreau or Grand Marnier, and whisk until mixture is glossy. Set aside.

In large bowl of electric mixer beat together eggs and sugar, starting at low speed until well combined, then beating at high speed for about 5 minutes, or until tripled in volume.

Add chocolate mixture to egg mixture and fold together gently with a large spatula just until incorporated. Fold in whipped cream gently, taking care not to deflate. Pour batter into prepared pan.

Place in a larger pan and pour hot water into larger pan to reach halfway up sides of smaller pan. Bake 30 minutes, during which time cake will rise and crack. Turn off heat and leave cake in the oven for 15 minutes. Remove from the oven, but leave cake in the water bath for another 15 to 20 minutes.

Turn gâteau out onto a flat serving plate, handling it very carefully as it breaks easily. Sprinkle with sifted powdered sugar. Serve with softly whipped cream.

Nowhere Café

8001 Beverly Boulevard, Los Angeles. 213-655-8895

Nowhere in the city will you find another Nowhere Café. This offspring of the famous Erewhon health food store, which has attracted health cultists since the 70's, has distilled a storehouse of health-food oddities – which may or may not appeal to most people – into something everyone will enjoy. Chef Robert Puchol uses kombu seaweed, silken tofu, wheatmeat, whole grains, California grain-fed poultry, and fresh seasonal produce and fish, all with imagination and flair. We enjoyed wheatmeat in a taco with other vegetables, served with tomatillo, and also in a Stroganoff. (Wheatmeat is textured and flavored protein derived from wheat sources.) A dish called Vegetables Oriental is an amalgam of colorful vegetables sautéed in a ginger-shiitake sauce. A meatless loaf of millet, pecans, and vegetables is accompanied by a savory country gravy. A turkey burger couldn't be tastier. A huge salad made of colorful vegetables cut like angel hair over greens is spectacular.

The furnishings are quiet; the atmosphere open and bright. There is good gallery art on the walls and cactus on every table. For those searching for a pocket of Los Angeles dining that represents serenity, grace, and wholesomeness, Nowhere is it.

Fresh foods, imaginatively prepared, are the stars on the menu, as the following chicken recipe testifies.

Grilled Chicken Breasts with Salsa Puchol 6 servings

The flavors of Latin America and Asia are combined in the very unusual sauce.

6   *small whole chicken breasts, boned, skinned, and fillets removed*

2   *tablespoons olive oil*

Salsa:

8   *ounces fresh tomatillos, husks removed, quartered*

½ small fresh jalapeño chile, seeds and membranes removed

2 tablespoons minced fresh coriander (cilantro)

½ small tart green apple, cored and diced (do not peel)

¼ small ripe avocado, peeled and diced

1 teaspoon minced fresh ginger

1 tablespoon fresh lime juice

   Sea salt and freshly ground black pepper to taste

Combine salsa ingredients in blender and puree briefly to a coarse consistency.

Brush chicken breasts with olive oil. Grill over medium-hot coals, turning so that a diamond pattern is formed from the grill marks on one side of the breast. Turn breasts over and grill a few minutes more, until just done.

Serve the breasts with salsa on the side.

Orleans

11705 National Boulevard, Los Angeles. 213-479-4187

Orleans is the best of the Louisiana-style restaurants that are a hot new trend in Los Angeles dining. Paul Prudhomme himself, king of Cajun-Creole cuisine, is a special menu consultant to head chef Thomas Blower, who once worked in Prudhomme's K-Paul's Louisiana Kitchen in New Orleans.

Los Angeles, long used to spicy dishes thanks to the proliferation of Mexican restaurants found in the Southland, has warmly embraced this style of cooking. Like Los Angeles cuisine, it is born of many nationalities: spicy Spanish seasoning, Italian oils, the culinary art of the French – mixed with the native American Indian and African influence, all stirred together with the natural skill of the people of the Louisiana bayous.

The original Creole cooking was created by the chefs of the wealthy French and Spanish aristocrats who settled in New Orleans and aspired to grand cuisine. Cajun cooking was hearty, pungent, and peppery, appealing to the strong, country-dwelling Cajuns, originating from French Canada. There are many similarities between the two cuisines, and the two terms gradually merged into something known simply as Cajun-Creole cuisine.

Orleans prides itself on the authenticity of its menu. Fresh seafood, especially Blackened Redfish, is featured on Orleans's menu, along with traditional hot and spicy Cajun-Creole dishes such as gumbo and homemade *boudin*. Jambalaya, a Cajun rice dish flavored with a combination of beef, pork, fowl, smoked sausage, ham, and/or seafood, is served in a moderate portion as an appetizer, surrounded by a flavorful Creole tomato sauce. "Cajun Popcorn with Sherry Sauce," another appetizer, is crawfish deep-fried in cornmeal batter with a spicy mayonnaise. Main courses include tasso (a Louisiana-style ham) and oysters in cream on fresh pasta and lamb chops seared on a hardwood broiler and served with mint jalapeño jelly and browned garlic butter. Dinners are accompanied by a basket of specialty breads fresh from the bakery: jalapeño cheese bread, molasses muffins, raisin bran muffins.

Following are two of the dishes we enjoy most: a superb sauce served over broiled swordfish, and a fantastic sweet potato pecan pie. Both are the inventions of Paul Prudhomme.

Hot Fanny Sauce About 4 servings

New Orleans chef Paul Prudhomme was inspired to create this sauce during a visit to his friend Alice Waters, chef of Chez Panisse in Berkeley. He named

it after Alice's new baby, Fanny. It is served at Orleans over broiled swordfish, or other types of white-fleshed fish such as halibut or sole.

¾ cup (1½ sticks) butter, chilled

6 tablespoons basic stock (see Note)

¼ cup chopped pecans, dry roasted

1 to 2 tablespoons Worcestershire sauce, or to taste

1 to 2 tablespoons seeded and minced fresh jalapeño pepper, or to taste

1 tablespoon fresh lemon juice

2 teaspoons minced garlic

Note: Basic stock at Orleans is made by adding any available vegetable trimmings (or 1 medium onion, unpeeled and quartered; 1 large garlic clove, unpeeled and quartered; and 1 celery stalk, chopped) and 1½ to 2 pounds beef shank or other beef, to about 2 quarts cold water and simmering for several hours. You may substitute any basic beef or veal stock – see Index.

Melt ½ stick butter in heavy 1-quart saucepan over medium-high heat, and brown until butter stops bubbling. Add all remaining ingredients except 1 stick butter, bring to a boil, and boil over medium-high heat until sauce is reduced approximately ⅓ its original volume, or until thick.

Cut remaining butter into pieces and add to sauce. Shake pan in a circular motion to incorporate butter, but do not let sauce boil. Remove from heat immediately and serve over broiled fish.

Sweet Potato Pecan Pie Makes one 8-inch pie

Two classic Southern pies combined in one wonderful recipe by Paul Prudhomme.

Pastry:

3   tablespoons unsalted butter, softened

2   tablespoons sugar

1/4   teaspoon salt

1/2   whole egg, vigorously beaten until frothy (reserve the other half for filling)

2   tablespoons cold milk

1   cup all-purpose flour

Sweet Potato Filling:

2   to 3 sweet potatoes (or enough to yield 1 cup cooked pulp), baked

1/4   cup firmly packed light brown sugar

2   tablespoons sugar

1/2   egg, vigorously beaten until frothy (reserved from pastry)

1   tablespoon heavy cream

1   tablespoon unsalted butter, softened

1   tablespoon vanilla

1/4   teaspoon salt

1/4   teaspoon cinnamon

1/8   teaspoon allspice

1/8   teaspoon freshly grated nutmeg

Pecan Pie Syrup:

3/4   cup dark corn syrup

2   small eggs

1 1/2   tablespoons unsalted butter, melted

2   teaspoons vanilla

   Pinch of salt

   Pinch of cinnamon

3/4   cup pecan pieces or halves

Sweetened whipped cream, to garnish

For pastry, combine softened butter, sugar, and salt in the bowl of an electric mixer and beat at high speed until creamy. Add egg and beat 30 seconds. Add milk and beat at high speed 2 minutes. Add flour and beat at medium speed 5 seconds, then at high speed just until blended, about 5 seconds more (overmixing will produce a tough dough). Remove dough from bowl and shape into a 5-inch disc about ½ inch thick. Lightly dust with flour and wrap in plastic; refrigerate at least 1 hour, preferably overnight, or up to 1 week. On a lightly floured surface roll out dough to a thickness of ⅛ to ¼ inch. Very lightly flour top of dough and fold it into quarters. Carefully transfer dough to a greased and floured 8-inch round *cake* pan (1½ inches deep) so that the corner of the folded dough is centered in pan. Unfold dough and arrange it to fit sides and bottom of pan; press firmly in place. Trim edges. Refrigerate 15 minutes.

For filling, combine all ingredients in bowl of electric mixer and beat at medium speed until smooth, about 2 to 3 minutes; do not overbeat. Set aside.

For syrup, combine all ingredients except pecans in mixing bowl. Mix thoroughly at slow speed of electric mixer until syrup is opaque, about 1 minute. Stir in pecans and set aside.

To assemble, preheat oven to 325°F. Spoon sweet potato filling evenly into dough-lined cake pan. Pour pecan syrup on top. Bake until knife inserted in center comes out clean, about 1¾ hours (pecans will rise to top of pie during baking).

Cool and serve with sweetened whipped cream. Store the pie at room temperature for the first 24 hours, then (in the unlikely event that any is left) refrigerate.

Palette

**8290 Santa Monica Boulevard, Los Angeles.
213-654-7045**

Palette, open for less than a year, promises to become one of the major Chinese restaurants in Los Angeles, if not the nation. The six master chefs from Shanghai, said to have prepared state banquets for Richard Nixon, Jimmy Carter, Henry Kissinger and Margaret Thatcher, among others, have the skill to reinterpret the epicurean opulence of Old China in modern terms.

The ingenious use of space from Palette's original warehouse proportions has turned the restaurant into a veritable palace. The decorating and lighting create the feel of a Fellini set.

The menu is in English, the dishes are elegant, but the connection is Chinese. Los Angeles diners have seen squab with pine nuts rolled in romaine in many other restaurants, but never as presented at Palette. Here the squab and pine nuts are delicate morsels rolled in radicchio. Noodles are offered, of course, but at Palette they take on an Italian twist: Linguine, not Chinese noodles, are topped with a saucy mushroom mixture. Another concession to Los Angeles taste is a spinach pasta topped with chicken and cilantro. Filet mignon, rarely seen on Chinese menus, is served at Palette sprinkled with chopped garlic.

One of the highlights of the menu is this spicy shrimp dish served in a sprightly cellophane package, bow-tied and all. The dish is brought to the table in its cellophane wrapping; the tie is snipped and the wrapping unfolded to reveal a steaming heap of rosy shrimp.

Spicy Shrimp in Cellophane 1 to 2 servings

20 *medium shrimp, heads removed*

Salt

1 egg white

1 teaspoon cornstarch

3 cups corn oil for deep-frying

1/2 teaspoon finely chopped fresh ginger

1/8 teaspoon minced garlic

1/8 teaspoon red chile paste

1/8 teaspoon hot bean paste

1/4 cup catsup

1 tablespoon sugar

Pinch of freshly ground white pepper

1/8 teaspoon white wine or dry Sherry

1/2 teaspoon chicken broth

1/2 teaspoon minced scallion

1 drop hot chile oil

1 drop sesame oil

Shell, devein, and butterfly shrimp. Rub shrimp with a pinch of salt, then rinse under cold water. Combine egg white and pinch of salt; add to shrimp and mix well. Add cornstarch and mix well. Heat wok over high heat. Add 3 cups corn oil and heat to about 350°F or until medium-hot. Add shrimp, and stir with slotted spoon for about 2 minutes, or until beginning to turn pink but not cooked through. Remove shrimp from wok. Drain off all but 1 table-spoon oil and return wok to heat until oil is very hot but not smoking. Add ginger and garlic and cook until garlic is light golden. Add chile paste and bean paste and stir-fry a few seconds. Add catsup and stir briefly, then add sugar, white pepper, wine, and chicken broth, stirring constantly.

Return shrimp to wok and stir-fry 30 seconds to heat through. Sprinkle with scallion, chile oil, and sesame oil.

Place a 16- to 18-inch square of cellophane on a 12-inch plate. Place shrimp in center of cellophane and tie packet closed with a red or other colorful ribbon. At the table, snip wrapping open and serve at once.

Note: The chefs use a heat-resistant cellophane purchased at floral supply stores.

Panache

444 North Harbor Boulevard, Fullerton.
714-526-6633

One of California's finest food emporia, Panache offers practically every known food item, down to ice cream made with soybeans. It epitomizes the food revolution taking place in America during the last decade: Middle-class Americans, inspired by travel and new culinary ideas, are spending millions in the pursuit of the ultimate culinary experience.

Panache, the creative inspiration of gourmet cooking teacher and food stylist Deborah DuShane, is fashioned after the European open-market concept, but no European open market ever looked like Panache. It's a stunning place with white marble floors, pine counters, neon clouds above white umbrellas – a bright spot in a huge office complex in suburbia.

The place is sectioned into specialty food areas. There is a gourmet-to-go bar offering pastas of every description, pizzas with unusual toppings, and innovative antipasti no Italian has probably seen before. The European-style deli offers imported cold meats, pâtés, cheeses from around the world, and caviar. The bakery features 12 different types of bagels and homemade croissants among the array of pastries. There is a coffee and espresso bar offering imported coffees and teas from around the globe. There is wine by the glassful for tasters, and beers galore. The ice cream bar fea-

tures Italian gelati as well as a soybean derivative – Tofutti, which made its way to California by way of New York. The restaurant tries to go Californian by serving up such things as baked salmon with yellow pepper sauce, veal with pesto, and fettuccine with escargots.

There are retail items from brandied raspberries to unusual chiles and vinegars, as well as cookware for the gourmet cook.

In other words, if you can't find it, Panache will probably have it. And if not, they will suggest a substitute ingredient and even make menu suggestions for a party – call their hot-line number 714-526-6635.

The following recipe is one of their most popular items in their deli case.

South American Spicy Chicken Salad 6 or more servings

Renowned restaurant designer George Lang has said that there is only one recipe for pasta salad but, unfortunately, no one has discovered it yet. This may be it – colorful and very Southwestern with its blend of chiles and cilantro.

1   *pound fusilli (corkscrew) noodles, cooked, drained, and rinsed in cold water*

12   *ounces boneless chicken, cut into 1-inch pieces*

2   *yellow bell peppers, seeds and membranes removed, diced*

1   *can (10 ounces) ripe olives, drained and sliced*

1   *medium tomato, halved, seeded, and diced*

1   *mild green chile (Anaheim), seeded and sliced (see Note)*

    Salt and freshly ground pepper to taste

Spicy Chile Sauce:

(makes 2½ cups, enough for 2 or more recipes)

1   *cup light olive oil*

½   *cup plus 2 tablespoons fresh lemon juice*

½   *cup fresh lime juice*

½   *cup coarsely chopped fresh coriander* (cilantro)

1   *medium tomato, coarsely chopped*

½   *small white onion*

2   *garlic cloves*

2   *Anaheim chiles, seeded*

1   *serrano chile, seeds and membranes removed*

1   *fresh jalapeño chile, seeds and membranes removed*

Note: It is not necessary to peel the chile.

Combine noodles, chicken, bell peppers, olives, tomato, and chile in a large bowl.

For sauce, combine all ingredients in a blender or food processor and blend until smooth.

Pour some of the dressing over the ingredients in the bowl to moisten the salad. Reserve leftover dressing for another use.

Il Ristorante Rex

627 South Olive Street, Los Angeles. 213-627-2300

Rex probably could not have happened anywhere but in Los Angeles. Rex is theater, a full-scale Cecil B. De Mille-scale production, and Mauro Vicente, a visionary who conceived the place and pulled it together, is the demanding, flamboyant director.

Rex occupies the restored ground and mezzanine floors of a former haberdashery in the Oviatt building, an Art Deco office structure built in 1928. Vicente

envisioned a revival of jazz-age opulence, spacious-ness and refinement. The hand-hewn floor-to-ceiling panels and chests of the old haberdashery have been restored to their original luster. The Lalique glass, gold-leaf columns, brocade walls, marble floors, lac-quered Art Deco furnishings are back.

There is no attempt at Los Angelesizing the *alta cucina* cooking by master chef Filippo Costa. It's classical modern Italian cooking at its best, and ingre-dients, largely imported from Italy, are chosen with no concern for expense; a rare truffle oil at $250 per case is used from some salads. Vicente has white truffles flown in from Alba regularly during truffle season. There is no freezer at Il Ristorante Rex, so nothing is stored, and the perishables are tossed out at the end of each day.

The antipasto is presented on a huge table at center stage, like a medieval banquet. But that's only for starters. The diner is cleverly coaxed into selecting both pasta and a main course. Not that the selections are hard to take: baby salmon served with basil sauce, sole with asparagus, New Zealand John Dory with tomatoes, eggplant, and green peppers.

But one should not stray from the pasta section. There is risotto (made with ox consomme); tagliatelle with dried Porcini mushrooms; lasagne with lamb sauce; ravioli stuffed with braised veal and served with butter-sage sauce; or the simplest of pastas – angel hair with fresh tomatoes, which Los Angeles diners have learned to enjoy lately. There is also this tagliolini with vegetables and a shaving of black truffles, served when truffles are fresh in season.

Tagliolini with Vegetables and Black Truffles 3 to 4 servings

This dish *is* a special occasion.

5	tablespoons butter
3	tablespoons mixed julienned carrots, celery, green beans, and asparagus
1⅓	cups heavy cream
6	ounces tagliolini or other pasta
	Freshly grated Parmesan cheese
1	small fresh black truffle

Melt 1 tablespoon butter in a large skillet. Add mixed julienned vegetables and sauté just until tender. Add cream and boil over high heat until reduced by half. Meanwhile, cook tagliolini in rapidly boiling salted water until al dente, about 3 minutes; drain. Add pasta to sauce in skillet. Add remaining 4 tablespoons butter, 2 tablespoons grated Parmesan cheese, and some grated or shaved truffle. Toss to incorporate pasta with sauce. Serve topped with remaining truffle, grated or shaved, and with additional grated Parmesan if desired.

Saint Estèphe

**2640 North Sepulveda Boulevard, Manhattan Beach.
213-545-1334**

"The natural products of New Mexico are nutritional and gastronomically excellent but only by transferring these products to a receptive environment such as Los Angeles can I create and present the unique dishes that are synonymous with Southwest Cuisine."
– John Sedlar

Whether or not Saint Estèphe would have happened elsewhere is hard to know, but chef John Sedlar thinks not. Los Angeles was the breeding ground for his training and ideas. The fact that Sedlar has virtually created a new cuisine based on French and Southwest cooking is due in large measure to his living and

working in Los Angeles, where experimentation, innovation, and creativity hold no bounds.

Sedlar's Santa Fe and French nouvelle cuisine is the result of his strong grounding in modern French cooking and his deep roots in the American Southwest. So there are tamales filled with salmon mousse, a fish terrine layered with green chiles, marinated veal chops with *sopaipillas* (fry-bread), and saddle of lamb with spinach and *posole* (hominy). Prawns are served with a bouillabaisse sauce flavored with *nopalitos* (cactus paddles) and chile pods. Fresh green chiles are stuffed with mushroom duxelles and served with a sauce of cream, garlic, and California goat cheese to make Sedlar's version of chiles rellenos. Even wines from Taos Valley are served along with fine French and California wines.

The fact that it is tucked into a neighborhood shopping mall in the out-of-way city of Manhattan Beach has done nothing to prevent St. Estèphe from commanding national attention. In fact, the Franco-Santa Fe recipes that follow have captivated such illustrious personalities as Craig Claiborne and master French chef Roger Vergé.

Green Chile Relleno Stuffed with Mushroom Duxelles, Served with Garlic Chèvre Sauce 6 servings

A first course that exemplifies John Sedlar's Franco-Santa Fe style of cooking.

6   *fresh mild green chiles (Anaheim, California, or poblano)*

1½   *pounds fresh mushrooms*

¼   *cup (½ stick) unsalted butter*

½   cup heavy cream

½   teaspoon salt

½   teaspoon freshly ground white pepper

Sauce:

2   tablespoons (¼ stick) unsalted butter

2   medium shallots, minced

1   tablespoon minced garlic

½   cup dry white wine

½   teaspoon salt

½   teaspoon freshly ground white pepper

2¼ cups heavy cream

5   ounces goat cheese, preferably California chèvre

Place chiles under broiler or in gas flame until skin is charred and blistered, turning to char evenly. Remove from broiler. Transfer chiles to a closed plastic bag to steam for at least 10 minutes. Remove from bag and peel off skin, wearing rubber gloves to prevent skin irritation. Rinse as necessary. Slit the chiles down one side. Most of the hotness is in the membranes and seeds, so remove those if you wish a milder flavor.

Clean the mushrooms by wiping with a damp towel and chop them finely, using a chef's knife or food processor. Melt butter in a heavy skillet over medium heat, add mushrooms, and cook, stirring often, until liquid is evaporated and they are quite dry. Add cream, salt, and white pepper and cook for 5 minutes or longer, until very thick. Divide the mushroom mixture among the chiles, spooning it inside through the slit. Wrap the chiles individually in plastic wrap and set aside.

To make the sauce, melt butter in a heavy saucepan over medium heat and sauté the shallots and garlic for a minute or so, taking care not to brown them. Add the wine, salt, and white pepper and cook until liquid is reduced to about half the original volume. Add the cream and goat cheese, bring to a simmer, and whisk until cheese is melted and smooth. Pass the sauce through a sieve.

To serve, place wrapped chiles on steamer rack and steam for 5 minutes. Spoon the sauce onto six warm serving plates. When chiles are done, remove the plastic wrap and place on top of sauce.

Blue Cornmeal Crêpes with Pumpkin Ice Cream 8 servings

Blue corn is a strain cultivated around the pueblos near Taos, New Mexico. It has a more delicate and slightly more bitter taste than white or yellow corn and a distinctive blue color, which is of religious importance to many American Indian tribes.

Crêpes:

2 eggs

1 cup finely ground blue cornmeal (see Note, Huevos Rancheros recipe)

1 cup milk

½ cup sugar

2 teaspoons unsalted butter, melted

Sauce:

½ cup sugar

1 cup fresh grapefruit juice

½ cup Grand Marnier

Garnish:

Rind of 4 grapefruits, removed with vegetable peeler

1 cup water

½   cup sugar

¼   cup fresh lemon juice

Pumpkin Ice Cream:

1   medium pumpkin (about 5 pounds)

3   cups heavy cream

1   cup milk

¾   cup sugar

4   egg yolks

For crêpes, beat eggs in a medium bowl until well combined. Blend in remaining ingredients. The mixture should be light and creamy; if thick, add a little more milk. Place a 6-inch omelet pan (preferably nonstick) over medium-high heat until a drop of water will dance on the surface. Wipe the pan with a paper towel dipped in melted butter. Using a 2-ounce ladle, pour in a little more than 1 ounce (2 tablespoons) of batter, rotating the pan quickly so that batter covers the bottom; the crêpe should be very thin. Cook until lightly browned on the bottom. Turn and cook second side about 1 minute longer. Turn out of the pan. Repeat with remaining batter to make 16 crêpes, buttering pan as necessary and stacking crêpes between squares of waxed paper.

For sauce, heat sugar in a heavy small saucepan over medium heat until melted and golden brown. Add grapefruit juice and Grand Marnier and cook until sauce is reduced to ¾ cup, about 10 minutes; it will be thick and syrupy.

For garnish, use a sharp knife to cut the rind into thin julienne. Place in a small saucepan with water, sugar and lemon juice, cook uncovered over medium heat until sauce is syrupy and rind has become semi-transparent.

For ice cream, cut pumpkin in 1-inch slices; place in shallow baking dish or roaster. Bake at 350°F approximately 45 minutes, or until tender. Scrape the pulp from the shell and puree in food processor blender until smooth. Transfer to a heavy saucepan and simmer over very low heat until quite thick, taking care not to scorch the mixture. Heat the cream, milk, and sugar in a heavy saucepan, stirring often, until hot. Whisk the yolks in a small bowl; whisk in some of the hot cream mixture. Pour the yolk mixture back into the remaining cream mixture, whisking constantly. Cook over medium heat, whisking, until the mixture thickens slightly and coats the back of a spoon; do not boil or the mixture will curdle. Strain. Add 2 cups of the pureed pumpkin to the custard. Freeze in an electric ice cream maker following manufacturer's directions.

To serve, place two crêpes, overlapping slightly, in the center of each of eight large serving plates. Place one scoop of pumpkin ice cream in the center of each crêpe. Pour sauce around the crêpes. Sprinkle grape-fruit rind garnish over the ice cream and crêpes.

Seventh Street Bistro

815 West 7th Street, Los Angeles. 213-627-1242

The Seventh Street Bistro is more than a beautiful restaurant; it's a legacy to Los Angeles. This stunning restaurant is housed in the restored Fine Arts building, erected in 1927 for Los Angeles artists who worked in its studios and exhibited their work in the exquisite Spanish Renaissance lobby. The restaurant is the brainchild of Wayne Ratkovich, a realtor dedicated to restoring beautiful old buildings in Los Angeles. Interior designer Brenda Levin could not have done a better job of maintaining the integrity of past and present. The place is breathtaking. And a meal at Seventh Street Bistro is as rarefied as you will find anywhere outside the Hôtel Negresco, Nice, where the very young executive chef, Laurent Quenioux, learned his craft. The cooking is continually changing, or, for a better word, evolving. What started out as a *ménu dégustation* of tiny sampling portions is slowly moving toward its original idea of bistro cooking – so if you crave pâté, you will find none better than that made at Seventh Street. Pâtés happen to be the passion of chef Laurent, and they are served either as a starter with a small clump of salad on the side, or in a terrine to end a meal.

Even the fixed-price menus include typical bistro dishes, such as French sea bass with artichoke sauce, Dover sole with salmon and watercress sauce, lamb loin with stuffed cherry tomatoes. Running through the menu one is bound to be somewhat startled by offerings like duck liver with blueberries, a cassoulet of apples with cinnamon, and the dish given here: fresh Pacific lobster medallions on a sea of pea puree laced with Champagne sauce.

Pacific Lobster with Pea Puree and Champagne Sauce 4 servings

A whole bottle of champagne in the sauce makes lobster even more of a celebration than it already is.

4 live lobsters (1½ pounds each)

2 pounds fresh peas, shelled, or 2 packages (10 ounces each) frozen peas

3 shallots, minced

1 bottle (750 ml) Champagne

3 tablespoons heavy cream

1½ cups (3 sticks) cold unsalted butter, cut into 1-table-spoon pieces

Salt and freshly ground black pepper

Snipped fresh chives or diced green or red bell pepper, to garnish

Bring a large pot of water to a vigorous boil. Plunge live lobsters into boiling water and cook for 8 minutes. Immediately plunge cooked lobsters into a pot filled with cold water to arrest cooking process; reserve cooking water to reheat lobster tails. Bring to a vigorous boil enough water to cover peas generously. Add peas and boil 2 minutes. Plunge into pot filled with cold water, then drain peas well; pat dry. Place peas in food processor or blender and puree until very smooth. Transfer puree to small saucepan and set aside. Break lobster shells. Remove tail meat and set aside. Discard shells.

Combine shallots and Champagne in large saucepan and boil until reduced by ¾ (to about 1 cup). Add cream and cook until sauce is reduced and thickened. Swirl in butter bit by bit, without letting sauce boil, until smooth and creamy. Strain sauce and keep warm in double boiler top over warm water, being careful to prevent further cooking.

Heat reserved lobster cooking water. Drop in lobster tails and heat through. Remove at once. Place pea puree in center of serving platter. Split lobster tails in halves and arrange over puree. Ladle butter sauce over lobster tails. Sprinkle with chives or diced pepper and serve.

72 Market St. Oyster Bar & Grill

72 Market Street, Venice. 213-392-8720

Owned by actor Tony Bill along with partners Dudley Moore and Liza Minnelli, this place is the newest Los Angeles celebrity hangout. Located in the heart of Venice, L.A.'s art community, it will probably remind most New Yorkers of Greenwich Village – right down to the wonderfully integrated art installations by fine local artists.

The cooking is American regional, with dishes like Cajun-style meat loaf and thick, meaty, hot Kick Ass Chili served with very good jalapeño corn bread. There is also derring-do cooking: steak tartare with fries, which because it is so contradictory actually works. We like their ideas: mesquite-grilled lamb and sliced Brie sandwich, grilled Louisana sausage with potatoes, grilled chicken with tomatillo salsa, grilled Hawaiian tuna with lemon and capers, and good garlicky spinach, garnished with roasted cloves of garlic.

72 Market St. is extraordinarily expensive for being such a casual place, but it's worth it for the experience of the offbeat menu and clientele – and an off-chance of Dudley Moore entertaining the diners from the grand piano that dominates the main room.

Ceviche, a marinated seafood cocktail long popular in California, is given a new twist with the addition of sea bass from New Zealand.

Sea Bass Ceviche 6 servings

Serve as a first course with or without fried corn tortilla chips.

8   ounces bay scallops

8   ounces New Zealand sea bass or any fresh bass

    Fresh lime juice to cover fish

1   tomato, halved, seeded, and finely diced

1   tablespoon finely chopped fresh coriander (cilantro)

1   tablespoon finely chopped fresh oregano

½   jalapeño chile, seeds and membranes removed, minced

¼   small onion, minced

    Salt and freshly ground black pepper

    Avocado slices and chopped scallion, to garnish

Place scallops in a bowl. Cut sea bass into small pieces the size of the scallops and add to bowl. Cover with lime juice. Add tomato, cilantro, oregano, chile, onion, and salt and pepper to taste. Toss. Cover and refrigerate for at least 2 hours.

Drain well. Serve chilled, garnished with avocado slices and chopped scallion.

Spago
8795 Sunset Boulevard, Los Angeles. 213-652-4025

Let's settle the mystery of the name right off the bat. *Spago* is the nickname for spaghetti, possibly because they serve pizza there, or because chef Wolfgang Puck loves ravioli. Does it matter? What does matter is that Spago is a legend in its own time, a pioneer in the development of the California-style restaurant. It's the creation of the culinary genius Puck, with a firm push from his artistic wife, Barbara Lazaroff.

What do you have at Spago that is different from its imitators or from anything you'll find in New York or Chicago? Puck style. Provocative ideas pop out of his head almost as if they were an afterthought. Who would think of lobster ravioli? Pizza with shiitake mushrooms and leeks? Liver with onion marmalade and mustard seed?

Puck was the first in Los Angeles to come up with an open kitchen containing a wood-burning brick oven, an inspiration, he says, from days working in southern France. There have been imitators galore since. Puck was the first to make use of pasta in his French cooking; there has been no end of French pasta-makers since. He was the first to loosen up nouvelle cuisine by turning it homey. He was among the first to introduce baby vegetables and encourage local specialty farmers to develop others. He'd travel miles for a brown pepper, and go anywhere for a good idea. The pizzas from Spago's brick oven were Puck's own idea. No elite

restaurant had dared serve lowly pizza before. His contained fillings that were…different…like this one, with salmon and caviar.

Pizza with Salmon and Caviar
Makes 4 pizzas

Small pizzas with fresh savory toppings are a first course specialty at Spago.

½   *recipe pizza dough (see below)*

¼   *cup extra-virgin olive oil*

½   *medium-size red onion, halved lengthwise, thinly sliced, and separated*

1   *tablespoon minced fresh dill*

⅓   *cup sour cream* or *crème fraîche*

Freshly ground black pepper

4   *ounces smoked salmon, sliced paper-thin*

4   *ounces golden caviar*

1   *ounce Sevruga caviar*

4   *small dill sprigs*

Preheat oven to 500°F *1 hour* before baking. Divide pizza dough into four equal portions. Shape each portion into an 8- to 9-inch circle. Place on pizza pans or large baking sheets. Brush dough with olive oil. Sprinkle with onion. Bake 8 to 12 minutes, or until golden brown, then remove from oven and keep warm. Meanwhile, mix dill, sour cream, and pepper to taste in a small bowl. Spread over each pizza. Arrange salmon slices over sour cream mixture. Spread golden caviar in a circle over salmon. Place Sevruga in center of pizzas. Garnish each pizza with a sprig of dill and serve.

Pizza Dough *(makes enough for 8- to 9-inch pizzas)*:

1   *package active dry yeast*

3   cup (about) warm water (105 to 115°F)

3   tablespoons sugar

2   tablespoons salt

4   cups all-purpose flour

½   cup semolina

¼   cup olive oil

Sprinkle yeast over ¼ cup warm water and stir to dissolve. Mix sugar and salt into remaining water in a small bowl. Combine flour and semolina in a large mixing bowl. Makes a well in center, add half the sugar mixture, and stir with a wooden spoon. Add olive oil and mix well. Add yeast mixture and mix 1 minute. Add a little more water if dough is dry. Turn dough out onto floured board and knead for 5 minutes, or so or until smooth. Place in an oiled bowl, cover, and let rest 10 to 15 minutes. Divide the dough into 4 equal parts and roll each into a smooth, tight ball. Place on baking sheet and cover with a damp towel for 1 hour. Use, refrigerate up to 6 hours, or wrap individually for freezer storage. (Thaw frozen dough overnight in refrigerator.)

385 North

385 North La Cienega Boulevard, Los Angeles.
213-657-3850

You could say that Los Angeles made 385 North. It's that offbeat, original, and straight out of Los Angeles, with its French-Japanese-American cooking and outer-space feeling. In fact, if it were not for the lively, down-to-earth bar scene, one would think one is dining on a satellite operated by extra-terrestials.

Roy Yamaguchi, the young superstar chef of 385 North, draws collectively from his multi-national experiences. Japanese philosophies of aestheticism and simplicity, his training in modern French cuisine

by master chefs in Los Angeles, and an American sense of improvisation and experimentation are all brought to play in Yamaguchi's cooking and inventive presentations.

What seems to be a typically nouvelle "composed" salad become an intricate embroidery of Japanese, French, and American ideas. Yamaguchi combines *gyoza*, a traditional Japanese panfried dumpling, with basil, Belgian endive, chicory, escarole, radicchio, and fruit (papaya and raspberries). The composition continues with slices of duck breasts fanned French-style over the salad.

You can be sure that dishes identified with Los Angeles (pastas and grilled things) will take on Oriental-Western tastes here. For instance, turkey is grilled to add to a salad of jícama and green beans. Curried salmon is teamed with papaya and hazelnuts in a Sherry vinaigrette. And in the pasta line, Yamaguchi sears prawns to add to pasta with tomato-basil sauce. We are particulary fond of this marianted squab pasta made with ginger, garlic, and black bean sauce.

Marinated Squab Pasta 4 servings

A combination of Asian and French flavorings enhanced by smoky Southwestern mesquite.

1   cup soy sauce

3   garlic cloves, minced or pressed

3   tablespoons plus 1 teaspoon grated fresh ginger

¼   cup sugar

1   tablespoon sesame oil

¼   cup olive oil

2   squabs, boned and split lengthwise

½   medium onion, chopped

1	red bell pepper, seeds and membranes removed, diced
1	green bell pepper, seeds and membranes removed, diced
¼	teaspoon minced garlic
¾	cup reduced veal stock (see Index)
1	tablespoon minced salted and fermented black beans (optional – see Note)
12	ounces egg noodles or other pasta, cooked
¼	cup (½ stick) unsalted butter
4	chives (6 inches each), to garnish

Note: Salted and fermented black beans are pungent in flavor. Roy recommends the least expensive ones, sold in Chinese markets in cardboard boxes, as they are the least salty. Rinse them well before using.

Prepare mesquite fire in barbecue. Combine soy sauce, 3 garlic cloves, 3 tablespoons grated ginger, sugar, and sesame oil in jar or bowl and mix well. Set aside.

Heat 2 tablespoons olive oil in large skillet over high heat until very hot. Add squab halves and sear, keeping meat rare inside. Remove from skillet. Pour soy sauce mixture into shallow pan just large enough to hold squabs. Add squabs and marinate 20 minutes, turning once or twice. Remove squabs, shaking off excess marinade; reserve marinade. Grill marinated squab halves to desired doneness over medium-hot mesquite on barbecue.

Heat remaining 2 tablespoons olive oil in large skillet over very high heat. Add onion, red and green peppers, ¼ teaspoon garlic, and 1 teaspoon ginger and cook until almost tender. Add veal stock and 2 tablespoons of the reserved marinade and bring to a simmer. Add black beans and noodles. Swirl in butter, coating noodles well; take care that sauce doesn't boil. Place noodles on platter. Slice cooked squabs and arrange over noodles. Garnish the top of each squab with a whole chive.

Tommy Tang's Siamese Café

7473 Melrose Avenue, Los Angeles. 213-651-1810

"One of the most significant influences in the Los Angeles food market today is unquestionably the Asian culture going back to the influx of Asian immigrants following the Vietnam War. Appreciation of foods from the Far East became increasingly popular. Today in L.A., Asian foods from Thai, Japanese, Chinese to Vietnamese, are combined with each other as well as with foods from other parts of the world."

– Tommy Tang

This is not your regular mom-and-pop ethnic Thai hut. It's a hip, super-attractive, cleverly merchandised and very comfortable eatery with innovative Thai food laced heavily with Chinese, Japanese, Indian, and Indonesian touches, which do, after all, mark the influences within Thai cuisine. You'll find Chinese shrimp toast, barbecued pork, egg roll, Indian satay curries, and Japanese tempura. There is brown rice, added as a health-conscious touch by owner, Tang. He has now added a sushi bar. Scouting those of Tokyo, he came up with master Sushi chef Toshi Sonohara, who, with Tang, has created offbeat sushis such as a California roll flecked with black and white sesame seed and a wonderful roll of paper-thin cucumber wrapped around eel and a mosaic of vegetables. Even the sushi bar appointments are tinged with Tang: There is a hot spice mixture made with chile, basil, garlic, and black sesame seed, similar to the Thai spice used at table, and a low-sodium soy sauce in a spouted jug – another one of Tang's health-conscious touches. There is talk that Tang has his eye on New York. Watch out, New York – you'll love it!

Tommy's Mee Krob and his Thai Toast are two of the most sought-after recipes in the city.

Mee Krob **6 servings**

1/4   cup fresh tamarind pulp (see Note)

     Oil for deep frying (about 5 cups)

5   ounces rice sticks

8   ounces ground pork

4   ounces small shrimp, shelled and deveined

1/4   cup rice vinegar

2   tablespoons sugar

1/2   teaspoon paprika

2   eggs, beaten

2   ounces bean sprouts

2   tablespoons chopped scallion

5   sprigs fresh coriander (cilantro), to garnish

Note: Tamarind is a legume with large brown seed pods. The pulp around the seeds is very sour and is used as commonly in Southeast Asian cooking as we use lemon juice. Discard seeds before measuring.

Soak tamarind in water to cover for 5 minutes. Drain, mash, and strain out seeds and fibers. Set aside.

Heat oil in wok or deep saucepan to about 375°F on frying thermometer.

Pull off a tuft of the rice sticks and loosen slightly. Drop into oil; noodles will puff and rise to the surface immediately. Use slotted spoons or large flat spatula to turn and cook other side briefly, but do not brown. Remove and drain on paper towels. Continue cooking remaining noodles in the same manner. Strain and reserve oil for another use.

Return 2 tablespoons oil to wok or skillet. Add pork and shrimp and sauté over medium-high heat until pork is browned. Add vinegar, sugar, paprika, and tamarind to skillet and cook over medium-high heat until a light syrup forms. Add the beaten eggs and cook as you would scrambled eggs. Remove from heat and cool for 5 minutes. Add noodles to pan and toss to coat well.

Mound on serving platter and top with bean sprouts, scallion, and cilantro sprigs.

Thai Toast 8 servings

Tommy introduced this Thai street-food favorite at his restaurant, adding his own inimitable touches, such as the tangy vegetable dip.

8	slices white or wheat toast
4	ounces ground pork
8	ounces peeled and deveined shrimp, diced
2	tablespoons chopped fresh coriander (cilantro)
1	tablespoon chopped scallion
1	teaspoon garlic powder
2	tablespoons Thai fish sauce (nam pla) (see Note)
1/2	teaspoon freshly ground black pepper
1	egg
1/2	cup vegetable oil
	Tommy's Tangy Dip (see below)

Note: This thin, salty, brown or brownish-grey flavoring agent is an important ingredient in Southeast Asia as soy sauce is in Japan and China. Many cooks consider the Thai version to be the finest. Fish sauces from Vietnam and Burma are very strong in flavor, and not likely to appeal to Western tastes. Tommy uses "Squid" brand fish sauce made by the Thai Fish Sauce Company, Ltd.

Cut each slice of bread in half diagonally. Cut bread halves into heart shapes with cookie cutter. Set aside.

Combine pork, shrimp, cilantro, scallion, garlic powder, fish sauce, pepper, and egg in a bowl. Mix well. Spread evenly over each bread heart.

Heat oil to 375°F in large skillet. Drop shrimp toast into hot oil, filling side down. Cook, turning several times to brown evenly on both sides, until golden brown. Remove and drain on paper towels. Serve with dip.

Tommy's Tangy Dip *(makes about ½ cup)*:

¼ cucumber, peeled and diced

1 tablespoon chopped red onion

1 tablespoon chopped scallion

2 teaspoon chopped fresh coriander (cilantro)

6 tablespoons vinegar

3 tablespoons water

2 tablespoons sugar

½ teaspoon plum sauce (see Note)

¼ teaspoon paprika

¼ teaspoon salt

1 tablespoon crushed peanuts

Note: Plum sauce, an amber-colored sauce sold in Asian markets that resembles mango chutney in flavor and consistency. It is sometimes called duck sauce because it is so often served with duck.

Place cucumber, red onion, scallion, and cilantro in a small serving bowl. Combine water, vinegar, sugar, plum sauce, paprika, and salt in another bowl and mix well. Pour over vegetables. Garnish with peanuts.

Trumps

8764 Melrose Avenue, Los Angeles. 213-855-1480

No restaurant better typifies Los Angeles. The look, cooking, the fun — it's all there. The place has an open, geometric simplicity associated with Southern California. The rooms, in beigy tones of light and bright, are furnished with built-in cement tables, extraordinary plants, and works of local artists. And if there is any doubt about where the Los Angeles elite go to see and be seen, try Trumps, whether for afternoon tea, a fund-raising lunch, or a meet-the-right-people dinner.

Perhaps the largest measure of credit should go to executive chef Michael Roberts, an American whose experimental cuisine is definitely of the California school. There is a bit of Oriental here, a touch of Southwestern or Mexican there, a hint of French and plenty of California improv. His nose for trends is uncanny. Even more uncanny is his knack of creating them. Roberts first dazzled his customers with an unexpected offering of potato pancakes and goat cheese. Then he created corn risotto with shiitake mushrooms, and the dual-personality salad that was part Oriental (raw seafood), part Mexican (salsa and tomatillos). He brought New York street food to Los Angeles with the introduction of the Cuban sandwich, except that his sandwich contained sautéed onions, goat cheese, and a meat salad. If you ordered pasta, there was no telling what the flavor would be. Grapefruit? Of course. And borrowing an Oriental knot motif, Roberts would knot strands of pasta and fry it. The recipe given here, a salad which combines asparagus and goat cheese with grapes and green peppercorn dressing, will give you a good idea of Roberts's daring.

Asparagus and Goat Cheese with Grape and Green Peppercorn Dressing 4 servings

Green peppercorns, which are simply undried peppercorns lend an intriguing, fresh, and rather pungent flavor to a warm salad of sauteed goat cheese and fresh asparagus.

1   can (2½ ounces) green peppercorns, drained, rinsed and blotted dry

2   cups seedless green grapes

½   cup vegetable oil

     Salt and freshly ground black pepper

8   ounces fresh asparagus

4   ounces goat cheese, cut into 1-ounce slices

2   eggs, beaten

1   cup fresh breadcrumbs

½   cup clarified butter

Place peppercorns in blender container and chop coarsely. Add grapes and chop finely. With machine running, slowly add oil and blend until smooth and thick. Season to taste with salt and pepper. Set dressing aside.

Trim asparagus and blanch in boiling water to cover for 2 minutes. Plunge into cold water to prevent further cooking. Drain. Dip cheese slices in beaten eggs, then roll in breadcrumbs. Heat butter in medium skillet over medium-high heat until hot; sauté cheese until golden brown. Arrange cheese slices on platter and garnish with asparagus. Pour dressing over cheese and serve immediately.

Valentino

3115 Pico Boulevard, Santa Monica. 213-829-4313

"The better restaurants of L.A. keep breeding more
restaurants, mostly creative, growing and challenging.
The fever of the city is the stimulation and the sophistication of our public gives us a possible audience,
a stage."   – Piero Selvaggio

Piero Selvaggio is probably the most tenacious restaurateur in town, always pushing himself, altering,
modifying, trying to give the fickle public what it wants.
And he's never satisfied. One gets the feeling he wants
to be on top of things at all times. And he is.

His stamp is personal service. Ask, and Selvaggio will
try his best to deliver. He is a youthful, handsome
Italian immigrant who was one of the first to introduce
classical Italian cooking to Los Angeles long before
most of us had any notion such a cuisine existed. While
he continually offers new and exciting ideas with
sauces, sausages, seafood, meats, and vegetables, he
rarely strays from the tried-and-true favorites upon
which his loyal following relies. There will always be
terrific calamari, linguine with red or white clam sauce,
and formidable osso buco, among other standbys.
Those looking for the unusual will find an excellent
risotto with radicchio that we have not seen elsewhere,
a shrimp salad with truffles, and a surprising steamed
veal. The list of up-to-date dishes from regional Italy
goes on and on, much like his wine list – which,
Selvaggio boasts, is the largest in Los Angeles.

The following is a *nuova cucina* first course featuring
a new cooking method, *en plastique*, in which a delicate food construction is poached in plastic wrap.

Petto di Pollo in Lattuga
(Chicken Breast Wrapped in Lettuce
and Poached in Plastic Wrap) 4 servings

This new cooking method will lend wings to your culinary creativity.

5   *chicken breast halves, boned and skinned*

2   *egg yolks*

1   *tablespoon chopped carrot*

1   *tablespoon chopped celery*

¼   *cup chilled heavy cream*

   Salt and freshly ground black pepper

   Pinch of freshly grated nutmeg

4   *romaine lettuce leaves, blanched for 30 seconds*

1   *cup water*

Port Wine Sauce:

1   *cup Port*

1   *shallot, minced*

2   *cups light cream (half and half)*

1   *tablespoon butter*

   Salt and freshly ground black pepper

Pound each of 4 chicken breast halves between pieces of waxed paper until thin. Place each breast half on a lettuce leaf. Set aside.

Cube remaining chicken breast half and place in blender or food processor with egg yolks, carrot, celery, cream, salt and pepper to taste, and nutmeg, and blend until smooth. Divide and spread filling equally over chicken breast halves. Tuck in sides and roll up chicken and lettuce jelly-roll fashion to form a roll. Secure seams with wooden picks if necessary. Wrap each roll in plastic wrap, twisting ends to seal.

Heat water in skillet, add chicken rolls, and simmer uncovered over low heat until chicken is tender, about 10 minutes.

Meanwhile, prepare sauce: Combine Port and shallot in large saucepan. Bring to boil and cook over medium heat for 3 minutes, or until mixture is almost dry. Gradually add half and half, stirring constantly. Simmer briskly until reduced to the desired sauce consistency. Whisk in butter until melted, taking care that sauce doesn't boil. Remove from heat and season to taste with salt and pepper.

Remove chicken rolls with slotted spoon. Unwrap and discard plastic. Cut lettuce-wrapped chicken into 1-inch crosswise slices. Spoon sauce into bottom of platter. Arrange lettuce-wrapped chicken rounds over the sauce. Serve with vegetables, as desired.

West Beach Café

60 North Venice Boulevard, Venice. 213-823-5396

The West Beach Café was doing California cuisine for a long time before all the recent attempts at defining it. Bruce Marder, the chef-owner, has for years been setting the trend toward the use of California products and interpretive American cooking – earmarks of the California school.

Marder's first major restaurant venture, Venice's Café California back in the early '70s, was followed by the opening of the West Beach Café, which became the laboratory for his creative cuisine. There were black-eyed peas and squid, pumpkin soup and curry-flavored croutons. Now the cuisine is moving toward Mexican-inspired interpretations: for example, pork stew with *posole* (hominy), topped with shredded cabbage and sliced radishes and eaten with corn tortillas. And who but Marder would think of filling golden blossoms of baby squash (when available) with Mexican refried beans, to serve with tacos stuffed with charred prime steak? American golden caviar is used here as a topping for medallions of Mexican sea bass. We asked Marder to come up with a recipe that said West Beach Café and Los Angeles in one breath. Here it is: fried California goat cheese served on a bed of California-grown black chanterelles and red-leaf lettuce.

Goat Cheese and Black Chanterelles
6 servings

Serve this flavorful combination as a first course or luncheon entree.

1   *cylinder (11 ounces) Montrachet-style goat cheese, cut into 12 slices*

1   *cup all-purpose flour*

2   *eggs*

¼   *cup milk*

2   *cups fresh white breadcrumbs*

½   *cup (1 stick) butter*

1   *pound fresh black chanterelles, quartered*

   Salt and freshly ground black pepper

1   *cup olive oil*

3   *heads baby red-leaf lettuce*

2   *tablespoons fresh savory leaves*

Dredge goat cheese slices in flour. Mix eggs with milk in shallow bowl. Dip floured goat cheese slices in egg mixture, then roll in breadcrumbs. Melt 2 tablespoons butter in medium skillet over medium-high heat.

Add chanterelles and sauté just until tender, about 2 minutes. Season to taste with salt and pepper; keep warm.

Heat olive oil in large skillet over medium-high heat. Add goat cheese slices and sauté, turning once, until browned on both sides. Remove from skillet and set aside.

Arrange red-leaf lettuce leaves on large platter. Arrange mushrooms on greens. Top with warm goat cheese. Scatter fresh savory leaves over salad. Melt remaining 6 tablespoons butter in skillet and cook until brown. Pour over salad. Season with salt and pepper.

Recipe Index

Salads
Asparagus and Goat Cheese with Grape and
    Green Peppercorn Dressing, 175
Chicken and Goat Cheese Salad, 140
Five-Leaf Salad, 73
Garden Salad with Fresh Corn and Balsamic
    Vinegar Dressing, 54
Paella Salad with Grilled Chorizo, 23
Pasta Primavera Salad, 72
Warm Sweetbread Salad with Snow Peas and
    Oyster Mushrooms, 123

Vegetables
Baby Butter Potatoes with Fresh Dill, 36
Carrot Flowers with Green Bean Stems, 43
Grilled Vegetables, 17
Mélange of Grilled Vegetables, 102
Roasted Yellow, Red, and Green Peppers, 58
Stir-Fried Vegetables in Fresh Herb Butter, 70